D0467889

# THE MORMON STORY

## A
## PICTORIAL ACCOUNT
## OF MORMONISM

by

**RULON S. HOWELLS**

ELEVENTH EDITION 1963
Copyright 1957, 1963, by Rulon S. Howells
All rights reserved.
Library of Congress Catalogue Card Number
57-14509

# BOOKCRAFT
### SALT LAKE CITY, UTAH

# PREFACE

PEOPLE all over the world are inquiring about the "Mormon" Church and its story. How did it start? Is it Christian? Do its members believe, worship and act as other religious peoples do?

To help answer such questions and inquiries, this material in the form of pictures, maps, and graphs has been assembled.

The principles, organization, functions and activities of this outstanding group of people are so different and varied that it is usually difficult for "outsiders" to understand.

To combine historical events with their locations on maps and to supplement with available pictures, it helps one to gain a more accurate and lasting impression of this fascinating people. The real name of their Church is "The Church of Jesus Christ of Latter-day Saints." The nickname "Mormon" has been given to them because in addition to the Bible they believe in the Book of Mormon, which is described as an American scripture.

The use of the word "Saints" or "Saint" in both the title of the Church (The Church of Jesus Christ of Latter-day Saints) and the designation of **all** of its members as Saints is used to designate those persons who have accepted the principles and doctrines of the Church, and have been baptized and confirmed as members of the Church. **All** members of this Church are designated as Latter-day Saints, or more commonly "Mormons."

During the ministry of Jesus Christ and for about two centuries thereafter, **all** those who were baptized into His Church were also called "Saints." Reference is made concerning **all** the members of the first or early Christian Church being called "Saints" in the following passages of the New Testament: Acts 9:13, 32, 41; Romans 1:7; 1 Cor. 1:2; Phil. 1:1.

They believe Jesus Christ to be the Saviour of the world and the chief cornerstone of the Church of Jesus Christ of Latter-day Saints. (Eph. 2:20)

Hofmann's famous painting of Jesus Christ

# Acknowledgments

THE AUTHOR gratefully acknowledges his indebtedness for photographs to the following: Committee on Radio and Television, and the Historian's Office and Library of the Church of Jesus Christ of Latter-day Saints; the Deseret Sunday School Union and the Improvement Era of the Church of Jesus Christ of Latter-day Saints; the Utah Tourist and Publicity Council; Glenn E. Nielson and Lloyd Taggart, Cody, Wyoming; the Salt Lake Chamber of Commerce; the Union Pacific Railroad; the Daughters of the Utah Pioneers; the Bureau of Information, Temple Square; S. Perry Lee, of the Church Section of the Deseret News; the Hal Rumel Studies; the Deseret News and Telegram; Lester F. Hewlett and J. Spencer Cornwall, Salt Lake Tabernacle Choir; Public Relations, University of Utah; the Gillham Advertising Agency; Sego Milk Products Co.; the Utah Photo Materials; Avard Fairbanks; the Brigham Young University Photo Studio; Otto Done; Ray G. Jones; Al Morton; Lionel McNeely; Dick and Mary Scopes; Howard R. Driggs, American Pioneer Trails Assn., Inc.

Also for help and information in graphs and charts: Jack Bytheway, Arben O. Clark, L.D.S. Church Welfare; O. Leroy Sanders and Dale Kilbourn of David W. Evans and Associates.

# Contents

# THE MORMON STORY

JOSEPH SMITH, JR., was born December 23, 1805 in Sharon, Vermont. His father was Joseph Smith, Sr., and his mother, Lucy Mack Smith. His ancestors on his father's side had for four generations come from Massachusetts. His great-great-great-grandfather was born in Topsfield, Mass., January 26, 1666. Beyond this his paternal ancestors came from England.

On his mother's side his ancestors came from Connecticut, and beyond this his maternal ancestors also came from England.

When Joseph Smith, Jr., was about ten years old his parents and family moved from Vermont to Palmyra, New York, in the northeastern part of the state, where they lived about four years and then moved to Manchester Township, New York.

The story of Joseph Smith, Jr., is a marvelous one and perhaps it is best to let him tell it in his own words.

**Picture opposite page**

**JOSEPH SMITH, JR. . . . . . the modern-day Prophet. Organizer and first President of the Church of Jesus Christ of Latter-day Saints.**

From a painting by Alvin Gittins

**THIS IS WHERE IT STARTED . . .**

The Sacred Grove, Smith Farm, Palmyra, New York State.

On the morning of a beautiful clear day early in the spring of 1820, a tremendously important and remarkable vision occured in this grove. Joseph Smith describes this great event in his own words on the following pages.

9

# JOSEPH SMITH'S OWN STORY

I WAS BORN in the year of our Lord one one thousand eight hundred and five, on the twenty-third day of December, in the town of Sharon, Windsor County, State of Vermont. My father, Joseph Smith, Sr., left the State of Vermont and moved to Palmyra, Ontario (now Wayne) County, in the State of New York, when I was in my tenth year, or therabouts. In about four years after my father's arrival in Palmyra, he moved with his family into Manchester, in the same County of Ontario.

Some time in the second year after our removal to Manchester, there was in the place where we lived an unusual excitement on the subject of religion. It commenced with the Methodists, but soon became general among all of the sects in that region. Indeed, the whole district seemed affected by it, and great multitudes united themselves to the different religious parties, which created no small stir and division amongst the people, some crying, "Lo here!" and others, "Lo there!" Some were contending for the Methodist faith, some for the Presbyterian, and some for the Baptist.

For notwithstanding the great love which the converts to these different faiths expressed at the time of their conversion, and the great zeal manifested by the respective clergy, who were active in getting up and promoting this extraordinary scene of religious feeling, in order to have everybody converted, as they were pleased to call it, let them join what sect they pleased — yet when the converts began to file off, some to one party and some to another, it was seen that the seemingly good feeling of both the priests and the converts were more pretended than real, for a scene of great confusion and bad feeling ensued, priest contending against priest and convert against convert, so that all good feelings one for another, if they ever had any, were entirely lost in the strife of words and a contest about opinions.

I was at this time in my fifteenth year. My father's family was proselyted to the Presbyterian faith, and four of them joined that church, namely—my mother, Lucy; my brothers Hyrum and Samuel Harrison; and my sister Sophronia.

During this time of great excitement, my mind was called up to serious reflection and great uneasiness; but though my feelings were deep and often poignant, still I kept myself aloof from all these parties, though I attended their several meetings as often as occasion would permit. In process of time my mind became somewhat partial to the Methodist Sect, and I felt some desire to be united with them; but so great were the confusion and strife among the different denominations, that it was impossible for a person young as I was, and so unacquainted with men and things, to come to any certain conclusion who was right and who was wrong.

My mind at times was greatly excited, the cry and tumult were so great and incessant.

In the midst of this war of words and tumult of opinions I often said to myself, What is to be done? Who of all these parties is right; or, are they all wrong together? If any one of them be right, which is it, and how shall I know it?

While I was laboring under the extreme difficulties caused by the contests of these parties of religionists, I was one day reading the Epistle of James, first chapter and fifth verse, which reads: **"If any of you lack wisdom, let him ask of God, that giveth to all men liberally, and upbraideth not; and it shall be given him."**

Never did any passage of scripture come with more power to the heart of man than this did at this time to mine. It seemed to enter with great force into every feeling of my heart. I reflected on it again and again, knowing that if any person needed wisdom from God, I did, for how to act I did not know, and unless I could get more wisdom than I then had, I would never know; for the teachers of religion of the different sects understood the same passage of scripture so differently as to destroy all confidence in settling the question by an appeal to the Bible.

## HIS FIRST VISION

At length I came to the conclusion that I must either remain in darkness and confusion, or else I must do as James directs, that is, ask of God. I at length came to the determination to ask of God, concluding that if He gave wisdom to them that lacked wisdom, and would give liberally, and not upbraid, I might venture.

So in accordance with this, my determination to ask of God, I retired to the woods to make the attempt. It was on the morning of a beautiful, clear day, early in the spring of eighteen hundred and twenty. It was the first time in my life that I had made such an attempt, for amidst all my anxieties I had never as yet made the attempt to pray vocally.

After I had retired to the place where I had previously designed to go, having looked around me, and finding myself alone, I kneeled down and began to offer up the desires of my heart to God. I had scarcely done so, when immediately I was seized upon by some power which entirely overcame me, and had such an astonishing influence over me as to bind my tongue so that I could not speak. Thick darkness gathered around me, and it seemed to me for a time as if I were doomed to sudden destruction.

But exerting all my power to call upon God to deliver me out of the power of this

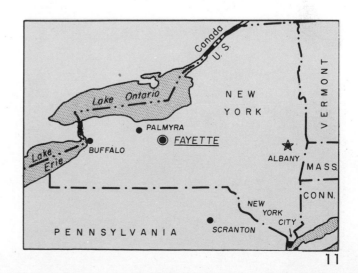

enemy which had seized upon me, and at the very moment when I was ready to sink to despair and abandon myself to destruction — not to an imaginary ruin, but to the power of some actual being from the unseen world, who had such marvelous power as I had never before felt in any being — just at this moment of great alarm, I saw a pillar of light exactly over my head, about the brightness of the sun, which descended gradually until it fell upon me.

It no sooner appeared than I found myself delivered from the enemy which held me bound. When the light rested upon me I saw two personages, whose brightness and glory defy all description, standing above me in the air. One of them spake unto me, calling me by name, and said — pointing to the other —

**"This is my Beloved Son, hear Him!"**

My object in going to inquire of the Lord was to know which of all the sects was right, that I might know which to join. No sooner, therefore, did I get possession of myself, so as to be able to speak, than I asked the personages who stood above me in the light, which of all the sects was right—and which I should join.

I was answered that I must join none of them, for they were all wrong and the per-

sonage who addressed me said that all their creeds were an abomination in His sight: that those professors were all corrupt; that "they draw near to me with their lips, but their hearts are far from me; they teach for doctrines the commandments of men, having a form of godliness, but they deny the power thereof."

He again forbade me to join with any of them; and many other things did He say unto me, which I cannot write at this time. When I came to myself again, I found myself lying on my back, looking up into heaven.

Some few days after I had this vision, I happened to be in company with one of the Methodist preachers, who was very active in the before-mentioned religious excitement, and, conversing with him on the subject of religion, I took occasion to give him an account of the vision which I had had. I was greatly surprised at his behavior; he treated my communication not only lightly, but with great contempt, saying it was all of the devil, that there were no such things as visions or revelations in these days, that all such things had ceased with the apostles, and that there would never be any more of them.

I soon found, however, that my telling the story had excited a great deal of prejudice against me among professors of religion, and was the cause of great persecution, which continued to increase; and though I was an obscure boy, only between fourteen and fifteen

**This is an artist's conception of the visitation of the two personages, God the Father and His Son Jesus Christ, to the boy Joseph Smith, Jr. This event occurred in a grove of trees on the Smith Farm early in the Spring of 1820. This picture is taken from a stained glass window in the Third Ward Chapel at Brigham City, Utah. Beautifully stained glass windows depicting this event are also to be found in several other Ward Chapels.**

**The details of this remarkable vision are given by Joseph Smith in his own words on these pages.**

The Hill Cumorah near Palmyra, New York, where Joseph Smith under divine direction, found the gold plates from which he translated the Book of Mormon.

## ... Joseph Smith's Own Story (cont.)

years of age, and my circumstances in life such as to make a boy of no consequence in the world, yet men of high standing would take notice sufficient to excite the public mind against me, and create a bitter persecution; and this was common among all the sects — all united to persecute me. . . .

However, it was nevertheless a fact that I had beheld a vision. I have thought since, that I felt much like Paul, when he made his defense before King Agrippa, and related the account of the vision he had when he saw a light, and heard a voice; but still there were but few who believed him; some said he was dishonest, others said he was mad; and he was ridiculed and reviled. But all this did not

destroy the reality of his vision. He had seen a vision, he knew he had, and all the persecution under heaven could not make it otherwise; and though they should persecute him unto death, yet he knew, and would know to the last breath, that he had both seen a light and heard a voice speaking unto him, and all the world could not make him think or believe otherwise.

So it was with me. I had actually seen a light, and in the midst of that light I saw two personages, and they did in reality speak to me; and though I was hated and persecuted for saying that I had seen a vision, yet it was true; and while they were persecuting me, reviling me, and speaking all manner of evil against me falsely for so saying, I was led to say in my heart, Why persecute me for telling the truth? I had actually seen a vision, and who am I that I can withstand God, or why does the world think to make me deny what I have actually seen? For I had seen a vision; I knew it, and I knew that God knew it, and I could not deny it, neither dared I do it, at least I knew that by so doing I would offend God and come under condemnation.

I had now got my mind satisfied so far as the sectarian world was concerned; that it was not my duty to join with any of them, but to continue as I was until further directed. I had found the testimony of James to be true, that a man who lacked wisdom might ask of God, and obtain, and not be upbraided.

Artist's conception of how the Gold Plates appeared, drawn in miniature after description given by Joseph Smith and others who had seen them.

**The Hill Cumorah as it looks today.**

L. A. Ramsey's painting of the Angel Moroni delivering the gold plates of the Book of Mormon to Joseph Smith, Jr., on September 22, 1827.

## THE BOOK OF MORMON STORY

**Joseph Smith, through whom, by the gift and power of God, the ancient scripture known as The Book of Mormon has been brought forth and translated into the English language, made personal and circumstantial record of the matter. He affirmed that during the night of September 21, 1823, he sought the Lord in fervent prayer, having previously received a divine manifestation of transcendent import. His account follows:**

WHILE I WAS thus in the act of calling upon God, I discovered a light appearing in my room, which continued to increase until the room was lighter than at noonday, when immediately a personage appeared at my bedside, standing in the air, for his feet did not touch the floor.

He had on a loose robe of most exquisite whiteness. It was a whiteness beyond anything earthly I had ever seen; nor do I believe that any earthly thing could be made to appear so exceedingly white and brilliant. His hands were naked, and his arms also, a little above the wrists, so, also, were his feet naked, as were his legs, a little above the ankles. His head and neck were bare. I could discover that he had no other clothing on but his robe, as it was open, so that I could see into his bosom.

Not only was his robe exceedingly white, but his whole person was glorious beyond description, and his countenance truly like lightning. The room was exceedingly light, but not so very bright as immediately around his person. When I first looked upon him I was afraid, but the fear soon left me.

He called me by name, and said unto me that he was a messenger sent from the presence of God to me, and that his name was Moroni; that God had a work for me to do; and that my name should be had for good and evil among all nations, kindreds and tongues, or that it should be both good and evil spoken of among all people.

He said there was a book deposited, written upon gold plates, giving an account of the former inhabitants of this continent, and the source from whence they sprang. He also said that the fulness of the everlasting Gospel was contained in it, as delivered by the Savior to the ancient inhabitants;

Also, that there were two stones in silver bows—and these stones, fastened to a breastplate, constituted what is called the Urim and Thummim — deposited with the plates; and the possession and use of these stones were what constituted "seers" in ancient or former times; and that God had prepared them for the purpose of translating the book.

After telling me these things, he commenced quoting the prophecies of the Old Testament. He first quoted part of the third chapter of Malachi, and he quoted also the fourth or last chapter of the same prophecy, though with a little variation from the way it reads in our Bibles. Instead of quoting the first verse as it reads in our books, he quoted it thus:

**"For behold, the day cometh that shall burn as an oven, and all the proud, yea, and all that do wickedly, shall burn as stubble; for they that come shall burn them, saith the Lord of Hosts, that it shall leave them neither root nor branch."**

And again he quoted the fifth verse, thus:

**"Behold, I will reveal unto you the Priesthood, by the hand of Elijah the Prophet, before the coming of the great and dreadful day of the Lord."**

He also quoted the next verse differently:

**"And he shall plant in the hearts of the children the promise made to the fathers, and the hearts of the children shall turn to their fathers; if it were not so, the whole earth would be utterly wasted at His coming."**

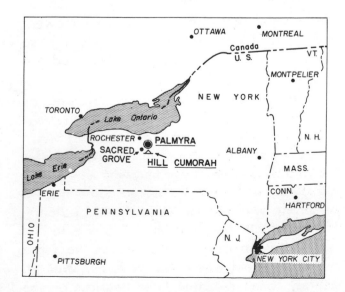

17

**Facsimile of characters on the gold plates from which the Book of Mormon was translated.**

## . . . Joseph Smith's Own Story (cont.)

Again he told me that when I got those plates of which he had spoken — for the time that they should be obtained was not yet fulfilled — I should not show them to any person; neither the breastplate with the Urim and Thummim; only to those to whom I should be commanded to show them; if I did I should be destroyed. While he was conversing with me about the plates, the vision was opened to my mind that I could see the place where the plates were deposited, and that so clearly and distinctly that I knew the place again when I visited it.

After this communication, I saw the light in the room begin to gather immediately around the person of him who had been speaking to me, and it continued to do so, until the room was again left dark, except just around him, when instantly I saw as it were, a conduit open right up into heaven, and he ascended till he entirely disappeared, and the room was left as it had been before this heavenly light had made its appearance.

I lay musing on the singularity of the scene and marveling greatly at what had been told to me by this extraordinary messenger; when, in the midst of my meditation, I suddenly discovered that my room was again beginning to get lighted, and in an instant, as it were, the same heavenly messenger was again by my bedside.

He commenced, and again related the very same things which he had done at his first visit, without the least variation; which having done, he informed me of great judgments which were coming upon the earth, with great desolations by famine, sword, and pestilence; and that these grievous judgments would come on the earth in this generation. Having

related these things, he again ascended as he had done before.

By this time, so deep were the impressions made on my mind, that sleep had fled from my eyes, and I lay overwhelmed in astonishment at what I had both seen and heard. But what was my surprise when again I beheld the same messenger at my bedside, and heard him rehearse or repeat over again to me the same things as before; and added a caution to me, telling me that Satan would try to tempt me, (in consequence of the indigent circumstances of my father's family,) to get the plates for the purpose of getting rich. This he forbade me, saying that I must have no other object in view in getting the plates but to glorify God, and must not be influenced by any other motive than that of building His Kingdom; otherwise I could not get them.

After this third visit he again ascended into heaven as before, and I was again left to ponder on the strangeness of what I had just experienced; when almost immediately after the heavenly messenger had ascended from me for the third time, the cock crowed, and I found that day was approaching, so that our interviews must have occupied the whole of that night.

I shortly after arose from my bed, and, as usual, went to the necessary labors of the day; but, in attempting to work as at other times, I found my strength so exhausted as to render me entirely unable. My father, who was laboring along with me, discovered something to be wrong with me, and told me to go home. I started with the intention of going to the house; but, in attempting to cross the fence out of the field where we were, my strength entirely failed me, and I fell helpless on the

## OLIVER COWDERY

A young school teacher 23 years of age when he acted as the scribe and wrote down nearly all of the translation of the Book of Mormon as the Prophet Joseph Smith dictated it to him. He was one of the three witnesses who saw the gold plates from which the Book of Mormon was translated. Although Oliver Cowdery later disassociated himself from the Church, he never denied his testimony of the divinity of the Book of Mormon. He was later rebaptized into the Church.

## DAVID WHITMER

A young farmer 24 years of age at the time he joined the Church. He was one of the three witnesses who personally saw the ancient gold plates from which the Book of Mormon was translated. He was also one of the original organizers of the Church. He was later excommunicated from the Church and although he never rejoined he did not deny his testimony of having seen the plates of the Book of Mormon.

## MARTIN HARRIS

A local farmer and business man 46 years of age when he assisted Joseph Smith with financial help and also acted as scribe for a short time in writing down the translation to a part of the Book of Mormon. He was one of the three witnesses who saw the gold plates from which the Book of Mormon was translated. He, like Oliver Cowdery, later disassociated himself from the Church but never denied his testimony of the divinity of the Book of Mormon. In his later years he was rebaptized into the Church.

**Joseph Smith used ancient Urim and Thummim in translating the Gold Plates.**

One account as to how the ancient records of the Book of Mormon were translated was given by David Whitmer, at whose home much of the translation of the Book of Mormon was done: "The Prophet, looking through the Urim and Thummim, would see appear in lieu of the strange characters upon the plates, their equivalent in English words. These he would repeat, and his scribe, separated from him by a curtain, would write them down. The scribe would then read the sentences written and if any mistake had been made, the characters would remain visible until corrected, when they would fade from sight to be replaced by another line."

## LUCY MACK SMITH

Joseph Smith's mother, who was a great comfort and support to him. She was born in Gilsum, New Hampshire, July 8, 1776, and died on May 5, 1855, at Nauvoo, Illinois.

## JOSEPH SMITH, SR.

The Prophet's father, born July 12, 1771, in Massachusetts. He was also a staunch supporter of his son Joseph. He held the position of Patriarch in the newly organized Church. He died in Commerce (later known as Nauvoo), September 14, 1840. No portrait of him is available.

## HYRUM SMITH

He was born at Turnbridge, Vermont, on February 9, 1800, and was five years older than his brother Joseph. He was one of Joseph's closest companions. He was killed by the same mob and at the same time as his brother Joseph, June 27, 1844, at Carthage, Illinois.

## EMMA SMITH

Wife of Joseph Smith the prophet, born July 10, 1804, Harmony, Pennsylvania. They were married January 18, 1827 and she died April 30, 1879, at Nauvoo, Illinis.

ground, and for a time was quite unconscious of anything.

The first thing that I can recollect was a voice speaking unto me, calling me by name. I looked up and beheld the same messenger standing over my head, surrounded by light as before. He then again related unto me all that he had related to me the previous night, and commanded me to go to my father and tell him of the vision and commandments which I had received.

I obeyed; I returned to my father in the field, and rehearsed the whole matter to him. He replied to me that it was of God, and he told me to go and do as commanded by the messenger. I left the field, and went to the place where the messenger had told me the plates were deposited; and owing to the distinctness of the vision which I had concerning it, I knew the place the instant that I arrived there.

### THE SACRED RECORD

Convenient to the village of Manchester, Ontario County, New York, stands a hill of considerable size, and the most elevated of any in the neighborhood. On the west side of this hill, not far from the top, under a stone of considerable size, lay the plates, deposited in a stone box. This stone was thick and rounding in the middle on the upper side, and thinner toward the edges, so that the middle part of it was visible above the ground, but the edge all around was covered with earth.

Having removed the earth, I obtained a lever, which I got fixed under the edge of the stone, and with a little exertion raised it up. I looked in, and there indeed did I behold the plates, the Urim and Thummim, and the breastplate, as stated by the messenger. The box in which they lay was formed by laying stones together in some kind of cement. In the bottom of the box were laid two stones crossways of the box, and on these stones lay the plates and other things with them.

I made an attempt to take them out, but was forbidden by the messenger, and was again informed that the time for bringing them forth had not yet arrived, neither would it, until four years from that time; but he told me that I should come to that place precisely in one year from that time, and that he would there meet with me, and that I should continue to do so until the time should come for obtaining the plates.

Accordingly, as I had been commanded, I went at the end of each year, and at each time I found the same messenger there, and received instructions and intelligence from him at each of our interviews, respecting what the Lord was going to do, and how and in what manner His Kingdom was to be conducted in the last days. . . .

At length the time arrived for obtaining the plates, the Urim and Thummim, and the breastplate. On the twenty-second day of September, one thousand eight hundred and tweny-seven, having gone as usual at the end of another year to the place where they were deposited, the same heavenly messenger delivered them up to me with this charge: that I should be responsible for them; that if I should let them go carelessly, or through any neglect of mine, I should be cut off; but that if I should use all my endeavors to preserve them, until he, the messenger, should call for them, they should be protected.

I soon found out the reason why I had received such strict charges to keep them safe, and why it was that the messenger had said that when I had done what was required at my hand, he would call for them. For no sooner was it known that I had them, than the most strenuous exertions were used to get them from me. Every stratagem that could be invented was resorted to for that purpose. The persecution became more bitter and severe than before, and multitudes were on the alert continually to get them from me if possible. But by the wisdom of God, they remained safe in my hands, until I had accomplished by them what was required at my hand. When, according to arrangements, the messenger called for them, I delivered them up to him; and he has them in his charge until this day, being the second of May, one thousand eight hundred and thirty-eight.

**Joseph Smith's home near Palmyra, New York. Near this home was located the "Sacred Grove" where Joseph Smith (at the age of 14 years) went to pray for wisdom, and in answer received the marvelous vision and visitation of the two personages, God the Father and Jesus Christ the Son, in the spring of 1820.**

21

## THE TESTIMONY OF THE THREE WITNESSES

BE IT KNOWN unto all nations, kindreds, tongues, and people unto whom this work shall come: that we, through the grace of God the Father, and our Lord Jesus Christ, have seen the plates which contain this record, which is a record of the people of Nephi, and also of the Lamanites, their brethren, and also of the people of Jared who came from the tower of which hath been spoken. And we also know that they have been translated by the gift and power of God, for His voice hath declared it unto us; wherefore we know of a surety that the work is true. And we also testify that we have seen the engravings which are upon the plates; and they have been shown unto us by the power of God, and not man. And we declare with words of soberness, that an angel of God came down from heaven, and he brought and laid before our eyes, that we beheld and saw the plates and the engravings thereon; and we know that it is by the grace of God the Father and our Lord Jesus Christ, that we beheld and bear record that these things are true. And it is marvelous in our eyes. Nevertheless, the voice of the Lord commanded us that we should bear record of it; wherefore, to be obedient unto the commandments of God, we bear testimony of these things. And we know that if we are faithful in Christ, we shall rid our garments of the blood of all men, and be found spotless before the judgment seat of Christ, and shall dwell with Him eternally in the heavens. And the honor be to the Father, and to the Son, and to the Holy Ghost, which is one God. Amen."

Oliver Cowdery
David Whitmer
Martin Harris

(Both of these pictures were taken from plaques on Angel Moroni Statue on top of Hill Cumorah.)

## THE TESTIMONY OF THE EIGHT WITNESSES

"BE IT KNOWN unto all nations, kindreds, tongues, and people unto whom this work shall come: that Joseph Smith, Jun., the translator of this work, has shown unto us the plates of which hath been spoken, which have the appearance of gold; and as many of the leaves as the said Smith has translated, we did handle with our hands; and we also saw the engravings thereon, all of which has the appearance of ancient work and of curious workmanship. And this we bear record, with words of soberness, that the said Smith has shown unto us, for we have seen and hefted, and know of a surety that the said Smith has got the plates of which we have spoken. And we give our names unto the world to witness unto the world that which we have seen. And we lie not, God bearing witness of it."

Christian Whitmer

Jacob Whitmer

Peter Whitmer, Jun.

John Whitmer

Hiram Page

Joseph Smith, Sen.

Hyrum Smith

Samuel H. Smith

23

# WHERE THE BOOK OF MORMON STORY TOOK PLACE...

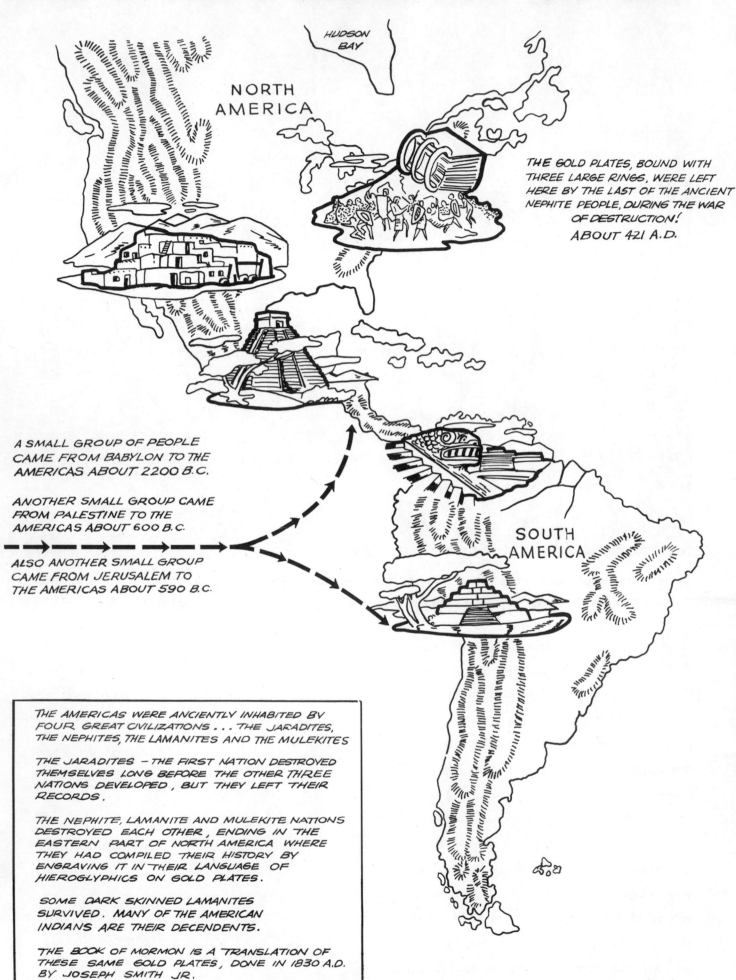

HUDSON BAY

NORTH AMERICA

THE GOLD PLATES, BOUND WITH THREE LARGE RINGS, WERE LEFT HERE BY THE LAST OF THE ANCIENT NEPHITE PEOPLE, DURING THE WAR OF DESTRUCTION! ABOUT 421 A.D.

A SMALL GROUP OF PEOPLE CAME FROM BABYLON TO THE AMERICAS ABOUT 2200 B.C.

ANOTHER SMALL GROUP CAME FROM PALESTINE TO THE AMERICAS ABOUT 600 B.C.

ALSO ANOTHER SMALL GROUP CAME FROM JERUSALEM TO THE AMERICAS ABOUT 590 B.C.

SOUTH AMERICA

THE AMERICAS WERE ANCIENTLY INHABITED BY FOUR GREAT CIVILIZATIONS ... THE JARADITES, THE NEPHITES, THE LAMANITES AND THE MULEKITES

THE JARADITES – THE FIRST NATION DESTROYED THEMSELVES LONG BEFORE THE OTHER THREE NATIONS DEVELOPED, BUT THEY LEFT THEIR RECORDS.

THE NEPHITE, LAMANITE AND MULEKITE NATIONS DESTROYED EACH OTHER, ENDING IN THE EASTERN PART OF NORTH AMERICA WHERE THEY HAD COMPILED THEIR HISTORY BY ENGRAVING IT IN THEIR LANGUAGE OF HIEROGLYPHICS ON GOLD PLATES.

SOME DARK SKINNED LAMANITES SURVIVED. MANY OF THE AMERICAN INDIANS ARE THEIR DECENDENTS.

THE BOOK OF MORMON IS A TRANSLATION OF THESE SAME GOLD PLATES, DONE IN 1830 A.D. BY JOSEPH SMITH JR.

# EXHORTATION OF MORONI

AND WHEN YE SHALL RECEIVE THESE THINGS, I WOULD EXHORT YOU, THAT YE WOULD ASK GOD, THE ETERNAL FATHER IN THE NAME OF CHRIST, IF THESE THINGS ARE NOT TRUE, AND IF YE SHALL ASK WITH A SINCERE HEART, WITH REAL INTENT, HAVING FAITH IN CHRIST, HE WILL MANIFEST THE TRUTH OF IT UNTO YOU BY THE POWER OF THE HOLY GHOST.

MORONI 10.4

From the plaque on Angel Moroni Statue on top of Hill Cumorah.

## THE BOOK OF MORMON HAS A PROMISE
### TO EVERYONE WHO WILL SINCERELY READ IT . . .

These words were written by Moroni, one of the last survivors of a great people of the Americas, about 420 A.D., during the time he was compiling the history of the ancient peoples who inhabited the American continent.

(Book of Mormon, Moroni 10:4)

25

## THE PRIESTHOOD RESTORED

WE STILL CONTINUED the work of translation (of the Book of Mormon), when, in the ensuing month (May, 1829), we on a certain day went into the woods to pray and inquire of the Lord respecting baptism for the remission of sins, that we found mentioned in the translation of the plates. While we were thus employed, praying and calling upon the Lord, a messenger from heaven descended in a cloud of light, and having laid his hands upon us, he ordained us, saying:

**"Upon you my fellow servants, in the name of Messiah, I confer the Priesthood of Aaron, which holds the keys of the ministering of angels, and of the Gospel of repentance, and of baptism by immersion for the remission of sins; and this shall never be taken again from the earth, until the sons of Levi do offer again an offering unto the Lord in righteousness."**

He said this Aaronic Priesthood had not the power of laying on hands for the gift of the Holy Ghost, but that this should be conferred on us hereafter; and he commanded us to go and be baptized, and gave us directions that I should baptize Oliver Cowdery, and that afterwards he should baptize me.

Accordingly we went and were baptized. I baptized him first, and afterward he baptized me, after which I laid my hands upon his head and ordained him to the Aaronic Priesthood, and afterwards he laid his hands on me and ordained me to the same priesthood — for so we were commanded.

The messenger who visited us on this occasion, and conferred this Priesthood upon us, said that his name was John, the same that is called John the Baptist in the New Testament, and that he acted under the direction of Peter, James and John, who held the keys of the Priesthood of Melchizedek, which Priesthood, he said, would in due time be conferred on us, and that I should be called the first Elder of the Church, and he (Oliver Cowdery) the sec-

26

ond. It was the fifteenth day of May, 1829, that we were ordained under the hand of this messenger, and baptized.

Immediately on our coming up out of the water after we had been baptized, we experienced great and glorious blessings from our Heavenly Father. No sooner had I baptized Oliver Cowdery, than the Holy Ghost fell upon him, and he stood up and prophesied many things which should shortly come to pass. And again, so soon as I had been baptized by him, I also had the spirit of prophecy, when, standing up, I prophesied concerning the rise of this Church, and many other things connected with the Church, and this generation of the children of men. We were filled with the Holy Ghost, and rejoiced in the God of our salvation.

Our minds being now enlightened, we began to have the scriptures laid open to our understandings, and the true meaning and intention of their more mysterious passages revealed unto us in a manner which we never could attain to previously, nor ever before had thought of.

**In the picture on the opposite page, the artist, Edward Grigware, has portrayed two closely-related events of great significance in the Mormon Church.**

**While Joseph Smith was translating the Book of Mormon, he and Oliver Cowdery came across the ceremony of baptism as recorded on the gold plates.**

**Baptism then, 1829, as now was misunderstood as to its form and purpose; so they inquired by praying to the Lord for enlightenment. On the 15th of May, 1829, they both went into the woods to pray for better understanding on this matter.**

**In response to their prayer, a heavenly messenger appeared to them and told them that he was John, known as "John the Baptist," the same man who, nearly 2,000 years ago, had baptized Jesus in the river Jordan. He laid his hands upon their heads and conferred upon them the Aaronic Priesthood, and then instructed them to baptize each other.**

**They accordingly went down into the waters of the Susquehanna River, Pennsylvania, where Joseph Smith first baptized Oliver Cowdery; then Oliver Cowdery baptized Joseph Smith. Each was immersed in the water after the true manner of baptism as was taught them by John.**

Copyright 1957 by Glenn E. Nielson,
Trustee in trust for the Cody Ward Mural Trust

Joseph Smith declared that Peter, James and John, apostles of Jesus Christ, who lived at the time of Jesus, came as resurrected persons and laid their hands upon the heads of Joseph and Oliver, ordaining them with special divine authority (the Melchizedek Priesthood). Thus they could act officially in God's name to perform ceremonies and ordinances and also to ordain other worthy men to act in the same capacity.

This tremendously important event took place on the banks of the Susquehanna River (picture and location map below) between Harmony, Susquehanna County, Pennsylvania, and Colesville, Broome County, New York.

At the right is the artist Maud Guibana's conception of the meeting held at the home of Peter Whitmer, Sr., at Fayette, Seneca County, New York, on April 6, 1830, to organize the Church of Jesus Christ of Latter-day Saints. Present, from left to right, were Joseph Smith, Samuel H. Smith, Hyrum Smith, David Whitmer, Peter Whitmer and Oliver Cowdery.

The Church, however, was not fully organized at this early date. The process of organization was gradual. New additions were made as required.

Joseph Smith at this time (April 6, 1830), was designated by revelation as a "Seer, a Translator, a Prophet, an Apostle of Jesus Christ, and an Elder of the Church through the will of God the Father and the grace of your Lord Jesus Christ."

Three years later the First Presidency, as now constituted, was organized. Then in 1835 the Quorum of the Twelve Apostles, next in authority to the First Presidency, was organized.

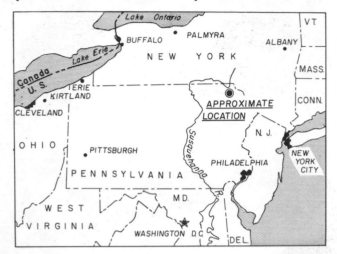

## THE CHURCH ESTABLISHED

Joseph Smith relates that, "Whilst the **Book of Mormon** was in the hands of the printer, we still continued to bear testimony and give information, as fast as we had opportunity; and also made known to our brethren that we had received a commandment to organize the Church; and accordingly we met together for that purpose at the house of Mr. Peter Whitmer, Sr., (being six in number) on Tuesday, the sixth of April, A. D., one thousand eight hundred and thirty. Having opened the meeting by solemn prayer to our Heavenly Father, we proceeded according to previous commandment, to call on our brethren to know whether they accepted us as their teachers in the things of the Kingdom of God, and whether they were satisfied that we should proceed and be organized as a church according to said commandment which we had received. To these several propositions they consented by a unanimous vote. I then laid my hands upon Oliver Cowdery, and ordained him an Elder of the "Church of Jesus Christ of Latter-day Saints"; after which, he ordained me also to the office of an Elder of said Church. We then took bread, blessed it, and brake it with them; also wine, blessed it, and drank it with them. We then laid our hands on each individual member of the Church present, that they might receive the gift of the Holy Ghost, and be confirmed members of the Church of Christ. The Holy Ghost was poured out upon us to a very great degree — some prophesied, whilst we all praised the Lord and rejoiced exceedingly."

(End of Joseph Smith's own story)

# Declaring the Old but Newly-Revealed Truths

JOSEPH SMITH was given the mandate by the Lord to share these glorious truths with all men. New concepts of old religious principles and new meaning and interpretation of the Bible must be explained to the world through missionary work. Joseph began with those around him who believed and helped him. Others heard and believed, and so the work spread.

The old but newly revealed Gospel of Jesus Christ that Joseph Smith was to share with his fellow men was the same as had been given to the "Jews" and "Gentiles" in Palestine and also to the ancient inhabitants (Nephites) in the Americas nearly 2000 years ago by Jesus Christ himself in person.

According to the Book of Mormon account, the American Indian is a descendant of a group who migrated from Babylonia and Palestine. The most important migration came to the Americas from Palestine, about 600 B.C.

The picture on the opposite page is a painting by the early Mormon artist, William T. Armitage, depicting "CHRIST'S GLORIOUS APPEARANCE AMONG THE NEPHITES," — ancient inhabitants of the Americas.

Jesus spoke of His "Other Sheep" whom He would visit. (John 10:16.)

Details of this visitation are recorded in the Book of Mormon.

**Below, an early day Mormon artist shows Joseph Smith preaching to the American Indians about 130 years ago. He is explaining their history as contained in the Book of Mormon. He is also declaring that they are descendants of the people depicted in the picture on the opposite page.**

# Nauvoo, Illinois

FROM THE TIME Joseph Smith received his marvelous vision, at the age of 14, until his untimely death at the hands of a vicious mob at the age of 39 (1844), the history of the Mormons is a long series of persecution.

The first large "gathering of the Saints" was in Kirtland, Ohio, where, by toil and sacrifice, they built a beautiful temple, only to be persecuted and driven from the area. The next stopping place was Missouri, but there was no rest there. Then they moved on to a swampland on the banks of the Mississippi River in Illinois. They drained it, beautified it, and built a city which they named Nauvoo. The city was laid out with broad streets running at right angles to each other, a model which Brigham Young followed in his colonization of the West. The state of Illinois granted the Nauvoo Charter, perhaps the most liberal charter ever granted to an American City. It provided complete independence in education, and in judicial and military branches in the government of the city. Within the short period of four years the Mormons had built a beautiful city, and had a university and a well-trained militia.

Here at Nauvoo, under the leadership and guidance of Joseph Smith, they toiled and sacrificed to build another beautiful temple. This was the last "permanent" home for the Mormons before their forced trek to the Rocky Mountains.

IN THE world's history, crusaders and religious reformers have all had persecutions to face. The Mormons were no exceptions. Since the time of Christ, for nearly two thousand years, no religious group had made such claims as these people made: their prophet had seen and talked with God; he had been given the restored knowledge of the Godhead — that God the Father, His Son Jesus Christ, and the Holy Ghost were three distinct and separate personages; he had been shown that man was created literally in the image of God; he had been told that no one in the so-called Christendom had divine authority.

Such declarations, new methods, new concepts and religious doctrines advanced during a period of religious intolerance, brought persecution in the worst form of mob violence to the Mormons. They were driven from one settlement to another. Their property and lands were taken from them, and their houses were burned. They fled from the persecutions of the mob.

The acceptance of these same new concepts brought a phenomenal growth in membership in both the United States and England, with the resultant gathering of its members to its headquarters in Ohio, Missouri and Illinois.

In order that they could live in peace and practice their religious ideals, they looked far to the West where there was plenty of land and few people.

The Nauvoo Temple, in ruins, tells a story of Mormon persecution. This Temple was built on the banks of the Mississippi River in the city of Nauvoo, which at the time, had a population greater than that of Chicago, Illinois.

# The Exodus from Nauvoo, Illinois

ANTI-MORMON sentiment grew. The killing of Joseph Smith seemed to intensify and accelerate the violence against the Mormons, who now realized that their religious practices and institutions were such that isolation was the only solution for peace and security.

Brigham Young saw, as did Joseph Smith, that the Mormons could not at that time of intolerance peacefully exist among other religious groups or denominations and still maintain and practice their own religious beliefs.

To avoid conflict and persecution, they would have to go far away from any other settlement.

Such a migration of thousands of families required preparation on a grand scale, and so during the winter of 1845-1846, with mob violence threatening Nauvoo, the Mormons,

under the leadership of Brigham Young, prepared for what they hoped and prayed would be their last great move — the trek to the Great Basin in the Rocky Mountains.

They knew they would have to build a new commonwealth hundreds of miles beyond the last American frontier. This meant they would have to take everything they needed with them, such as tools, farming implements, seed, cattle and clothing.

Very early in 1846 thousands of Mormons left Nauvoo for the West. This was the start of one of history's most remarkable migrations.

**The artist, Edward Grigware, depicts the burning of Nauvoo and the fleeing of the surviving Mormons from the city.**

**Mormons crossing the frozen Mississippi River from the Nauvoo side to the Iowa banks.**

**by J. Leo Fairbanks**

Copyright 1957 by Glenn E. Nielson,
Trustee in trust for the Cody Ward Mural Trust

JOSEPH SMITH and his brother Hyrum, who was very close to him in his work, were both killed by a mob on June 27, 1844. Joseph Smith was then 39 years old and his brother Hyrum 44 years old.

Brigham Young, as senior member and President of the Quorum of the Twelve Apostles, succeeded Joseph Smith as leader of the Church.

Brigham Young was born in the State of Vermont on June 1, 1801. At the time he was baptized and became a member of the Church, on April 14, 1832, he was a carpenter, joiner, painter and glazier. He was soon called to be an Apostle of the Church.

The enemies of Mormonism thought that when Joseph Smith was out of the way the Church would fall to pieces. They knew little of the courage, ability and leadership of Brigham Young, and of other inspired leaders of the Church.

**Carthage Jail where Joseph and Hyrum Smith were killed.**

**BRIGHAM YOUNG** — This picture was taken about the time he became President and leader of the Church at the age of 43. He succeeded Joseph Smith, who was killed by a mob at Carthage, Illinois, on June 27, 1844.

**MORMON EXODUS IN WINTER**                    by Edward Grigware

Copyright 1957 by Glenn E. Nielson,
Trustee in trust for the Cody Ward Mural Trust

# Westward to a Far-away Land

ALMOST TWO YEARS before the first Mormon Pioneers had crossed the desert wilderness westward to the Rocky Mountains, the place of their refuge was determined — a place uninviting and unattractive to others, but a place they sought where they would live in peace and develop their own form of commonwealth.

The causes of the Mormon expulsion from Ohio, Missouri and from Illinois, were many. The Mormons were industrious. Large numbers of their members settled together in the area where by co-operative effort they could build a temple and live among those having the same philosophy, religious beliefs and practices. In a frontier country this aggressive and well-organized program developed jealousies among many non-Mormons struggling by themselves, only to be overshadowed in the tremendous accomplishments that the "help-one-another" co-operative Mormon program made. Religious intolerance grew among so-called Christian groups, who, because of losing followers to the aggressive Mormon proselyting efforts, added fuel to the flame of persecution.

In the short time of four years, a semi-swamp land on the banks of the Mississippi River had been transformed into Illinois' largest and most attractive city, with a Temple building more imposing in size and structure than any other building west of the Allegheny Mountains. This was Nauvoo.

All this they had to abandon. Temple, homes, business and farms, all had to be left behind as they turned westward toward what to them was an uncharted wilderness. Since mob violence was increasing, they hurriedly made preparations by trading homes, farms and anything they had for wagons, oxen, horses and provisions to take with them in their westward flight. They set up shops to make most of their equipment — tents, wagons, etc.

The "Exodus" started on February 4th, 1846, with six hundred Saints crossing the Mississippi River on ice. By September of 1846 all had left Nauvoo but 150 men and a few women and children unable to leave because of sickness. Even these few remaining were later driven out.

The "Exodus" from Nauvoo and the migration westward, as seen through the eyes of a celebrated historian, H. H. Bancroft, is graphically depicted in the following account:

**THE TREK**                                **by J. Leo Fairbanks**

**ON THE TREK WESTWARD**                                    **by William H. Jackson**

"There is no parallel in the world's history to this migration from Nauvoo. The exodus from Egypt was from a heathen land, a land of idolators, to a fertile region designated by the Lord for His chosen people, the land of Canaan. The Pilgrim fathers, in fleeing to America, came from a bigoted and despotic people — a people making few pretentions to civil or religious liberty. It was from these same people who had fled from old-world persecutions that they might enjoy liberty of conscience in the wilds of America, from their descendants and associates, that others of their descendants, who claimed the right to differ from them in opinion and practice, were now fleeing . . . . Before this the Mormons had been driven to the outskirts of civilization, where they had built themselves a city; this they must now abandon, and throw themselves upon the mercy of savages."

W. E. Woodward, another historian, records the following:

"They were inspired by the thought of the departure of the children of Israel from Egypt in search of a Promised Land. Were not the Mormons the new Israelites, and was not Brigham Young a reincarnation of Moses: Like the Israelites of that ancient time they carried with them the precious words of God. It was the most dramatic emigration of a body of people that has ever occurred in our history."

A vivid description of the conditions under which the Mormons were forced to travel as they left Nauvoo and crossed the Missouri to Iowa was given by Eliza R. Snow, who visited the first Mormon camps along the trail in the Iowa territory.

"We had been preceded (from Nauvoo) by thousands, and I was informed that on the

first night of the encampment, nine children were born into the world, and from that time, as we journeyed onward, mothers gave birth to offspring under almost every variety of circumstances imaginable, except those to which they had been accustomed; some in tents, others in wagons — in rainstorms and in snowstorms.

"Let it be remembered that the mothers of these wilderness-born babies were not savages, accustomed to roam the forest and brave the storm and tempest — most of them were born and educated in the Eastern States, and under trying circumstances had assisted, by their faith, patience and energies, in making Nauvoo what its name indicates, 'the Beautiful.' There they had lovely homes, decorated with flowers and enriched with choice fruit trees, just beginning to yield plentifully.

"To these homes, without lease or sale, they had just bade a final adieu, and with what little of their substance could be packed into

one, two, and in some instances, three wagons, had started out, desertward, for . . . where? To this question the only response at that time was 'God knows.' "

The first encampment, after leaving the west bank of the Mississippi, was on Sugar Creek, in Iowa territory, about nine miles from Nauvoo.

Under pressure of threatened mob attack, the first group of pioneers had left Nauvoo in February, then others in March. All departed in haste and with inadequate supplies. The weather was bitter cold. Many of the groups were able to cross the Mississippi River on its frozen surface; others a little later crossed on skiffs and barges, with huge cakes of broken ice jamming against their overloaded frail barges and rafts.

In April and May severe storms kept them huddled in camp for days at a time. Suffering was intense, and deaths from exposure, disease and malnutrition were many.

**A PIONEER ENCAMPMENT**                                      **by William H. Jackson**

As soon as spring warmed the soil enough to plant, acres of ground were fenced, broken and planted at settlements along the way so that those coming later could reap the harvest and be helped.

In late June, 1846, Council Bluffs on the Missouri River was reached by the advance group. This place was designated as temporary headquarters.

As the various camps moved across Iowa, it was customary to send out an advance company called "pioneers," who blazed the trail to be followed by the wagons. Sometimes they detailed a squad from their company to build a bridge or clear a way through the underbrush of the timber tracts they crossed; while others would be detailed to find a suitable encampment. Trading or foraging expeditions were sent out to scour the country for corn and cattle, in exchange for cash and household goods, table furnishings, feather beds, silverware, etc. Other parties

were sent out to make labor contracts in order that many of the Pioneers could earn money to help buy needed equipment and supplies.

After crossing Iowa, the first advanced groups of pioneers made temporary headquarters for the winter of 1846-1847 on the bank of the Missouri River, where the city of Omaha, Nebraska, now stands.

Here in their "winter quarters" they weathered the storms of the severe winter, preparing for spring when they could plant gardens to leave behind them for the help of others to follow. Then they started out early to blaze the trail to the Rocky Mountains.

Along the way from Nauvoo to the Missouri, other temporary settlements had been made at Sugar City, Garden Grove, Mount Pisgah and Council Bluffs. In each of these places hundreds of acres of land had been fenced, cultivated and planted, houses erected and everything done within the meager means of the Pioneers to make a welcome resting place or winter encampment for other groups who would be on the trail later. For many years after, emigrants from Europe and other converts traveling to the Rocky Mountains found refuge and help in these settlements along the trail in Iowa.

The trek across Iowa is vividly described by one of the pioneer women who made the journey. She said: "When hearing the rehearsal of trials, privations and hardships endured by the camps of Israel, while journeying from the Mississippi River to the Missouri, my mind inadvertently turns to that portion between Nauvoo and Garden Grove, as the darkest in my memory. We were poorly prepared for such an exodus; and many joining us who were anxious to come, but had little or nothing of the necessaries for their own sustenance, our meager rations had to be divided among them. We had many weeks of cold, stormy weather, and our teams being insufficient to draw the loads, rendered traveling over those soft prairies next thing to an impossibility; expecting, as we did, to go over the mountains that year, we were put on rations, and had to lengthen out our flour and provisions in the most economical manner. During that time our sea biscuit, crackers, parched corn meal, etc., which were among the luxuries, molded, until finally they were fed to our horses and cattle. At the beginning of the journey the crackers went very well to eat dry, but I'll never forget the first time I saw a meal made of sea biscuit broken into milk. I had called at Uncle Brigham's tent — I had always addressed him by that title — where he was just taking some for dinner, and he invited me to have a bowl; but I declined, with thanks, and a feeling of wonder as to how he could relish it. When it came to sitting down daily to milk and water porridge with crackers in it, it became so nauseous that hunger could not tempt me to eat it.

"At this period the young, and even aged people were forced to walk, if it were possible, a goodly portion of the way to save the teams; no matter what the weather might be, storms or excessive heat, or how weary, faint and footsore they became, there was no alternative but to endure 'till they had reached the spot called Garden Grove. Here they unpacked and sent out many valuables into the Missouri settlements and exchanged them for provisions and the most needful articles. They also traded horses for oxen and milch cows, and from that time our living was more comfortable."

**During that terrible winter of 1846-1847 at Winter Quarters, more than 600 pioneers died of hunger and exposure. This tragedy is expressed in the imposing monument done by Avard Fairbanks. It is now located at Winter Quarters Cemetery near Omaha, Nebraska.**

# Some Went By Water . . .

ON FEBRUARY 4, 1846, the first refugees left Nauvoo and crossed the Mississippi River going west; also on that same day the ship Brooklyn left New York harbor with 235 Mormons bound for California and the West. The vessel of four hundred fifty ton size had been chartered by Samuel Brannon, as leader of the group, for $1,200 a month.

Some of the members of the Church living in the eastern states thought that rather than to make the trek across the continent, it would be easier to go by ship to the West Coast and then by land to the place designated in the Rocky Mountains, and so they gathered in New York and set sail on February 4, 1846, bound for San Francisco, California.

Each adult person was charged $75.00 for transportation and board. They took with them agricultural and mechanical tools, implements and equipment, including plows, shovels, spades, scythes, sickles, nails, glass, blacksmith and carpenter equipment, material for three grain mills, a printing press, twine, various metals and assorted cattle. They also took a large quantity of school books, including spelling, history, arithmetic, astronomy, geography and Hebrew grammar books. They sailed around South America, and after touching at the Island of Juan Fernandez and at Honolulu in the Hawaiian Islands, they arrived at Yerba Buena (now San Francisco) on July 31, 1846, having sailed from New York five months and twenty-seven days earlier.

Sam Brannon, their leader, then went with two guides by horseback to the Rocky Mountains to meet Brigham Young and try to persuade him to bring all the rest of the Mormons on to California. Brigham Young knew that if he led them to California they could never have the peace and isolation that the Rocky Mountains offered. Brannon failed in the attempt to persuade Brigham Young. He returned to California where he amassed a fortune, but he estranged himself from the Church and finally died a pauper in Southern California. Most of the members who sailed with him finally joined the main body in the valley of the Great Salt Lake.

* * *

THE ABILITY of Brigham Young, as the leader, to unify the sorely-tried people as they attempted to make camps along the trail in Iowa territory was remarkable.

At Sugar Creek, Iowa, the first camp was made. This was on the Iowa side of the Mississippi River, which at the time was flowing with huge ice cakes, making it even more difficult to cross. No sooner had they made camp than men were assigned to go ahead and find sites for subsequent camps farther west. Others were to go into neighboring communities to buy grain, and to work so they could obtain provisions. All was organized to the end that those who followed would be at least partially taken care of.

It was cold, fresh snow had fallen, food was scarce, but amid all of these trying circumstances they kept up their spirits with festivities in the form of song, instrumental music, dancing and humorous readings. Their instrumental band was invited into other communities in Iowa to entertain, the proceeds going to purchase foodstuffs, wagons, oxen, milch cows and other necessities. Surely they made the best of every situation.

**THE POSTOFFICE OF THE PRAIRIES**
**by Frank Nebeker**
(Notes were left in buffalo skulls.)

## THE UNITED STATES GOVERNMENT ENLISTS

# A Mormon Battalion

ON JULY 1, 1846, at Council Bluffs, President Brigham Young introduced Captain James Allen of the United States Army to the people who had gathered to hear the captain's message. An order had been given by President James K. Polk to enlist men among the Mormons to take part in the war against Mexico.

Five hundred able-bodied men were requested by the United States, and these, too, in the heart of an Indian country, "in the midst of an exodus unparalleled for dangers and hardships, when every man was needed for defense and when because of the scarcity of men, even delicate women had been seen driving teams and tending stock."

And yet the call had its advantages. The charge had repeatedly been made that the Mormons were disloyal to the American government. Here was an opportunity to vindicate themselves. To enter the service of the government in time of war would be an evidence of loyalty that would stand both unimpeached and unimpeachable.

The Mormons were to join as volunteers under special privileges. They were to choose their own officers, receive gratis their guns and equipment to be furnished them at Fort Leavenworth. The Battalion's pay was to go to their families in helping to equip them for the trek to the Great Salt Lake Valley.

The Mormon Battalion, participating in the Mexican campaign for California, materially aided in the conquest of the West and the very fact the Mexicans were aware that an "Army" of the United States was marching toward California, no doubt accelerated the treaty of Cahuenga, January 13, 1847.

In crossing the coast range of mountains the men of the Battalion found it necessary in some places to convey the wagons over the steep incline by means of ropes, and where the trail was too narrow, to take the wagons apart and carry them over piece by piece.

The Battalion's march made a southern route for the transcontinental railroad that came later.

After discharge, the members of the Battalion brought back to the Great Salt Lake Valley seeds of many kinds, especially much-needed wheat, and added greatly to Mormon communities of Utah by bringing back with them wagons, horses, mules, cattle and ammunition.

Nine of the twelve men who were with James Marshall in the Coloma Valley constructing Sutter's Sawmill when gold was discovered, January 24, 1848, had belonged to the Battalion. The rich areas known as "Mormon Island" and "Mormon Diggins," discovered by Battalion men, became famous and did much to spread the news of the gold discovery.

Perhaps the greatest service to the Mormon cause made by the Battalion was removing much of the prejudice against the Mormons and displaying the loyalty the Mormons felt toward the Government of the United States.

The march of the Mormon Battalion from Council Bluffs, Iowa, to San Diego, California, over 2,000 miles, is credited with being the longest march of infantry in military history.

After they were discharged, some of the Battalion members remained in California to work, but most of them journeyed to Salt Lake to join the main body of the Church.

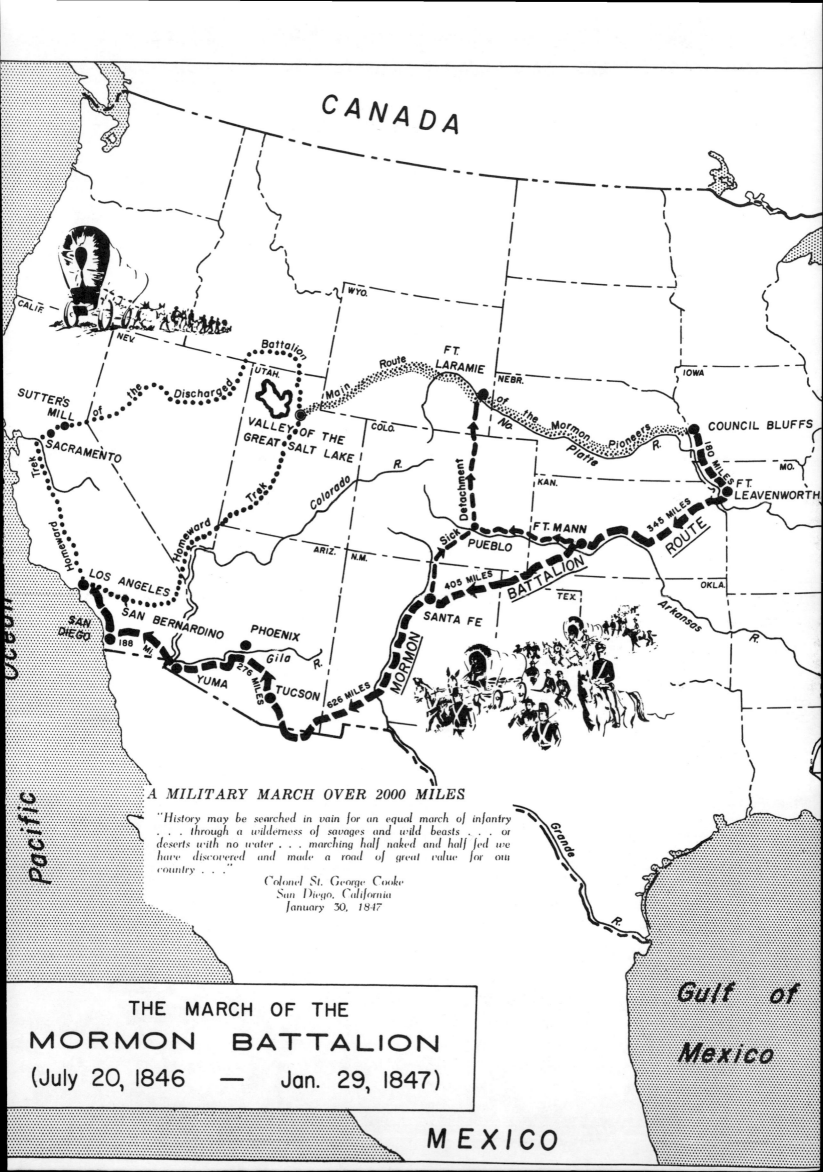

CANADA

CALIF.

NEV.

Battalion

Discharged

UTAH.

Main

Route

FT.
LARAMIE

NEBR.

IOWA

SUTTER'S
MILL

of
the

VALLEY OF THE
GREAT SALT LAKE

of
the
Mormon

Pioneers

COUNCIL BLUFFS

SACRAMENTO

COLO.

Platte
R.

MO.

180 MILES

Trek

Homeward
Trek

Colorado
R.

KAN.

FT.
LEAVENWORTH

Homeward

Sick
Detachment

PUEBLO

FT. MANN

345 MILES

ROUTE

LOS ANGELES

ARIZ.

N.M.

405 MILES

BATTALION

OKLA.

SAN
DIEGO

SAN BERNARDINO

PHOENIX

SANTA FE

TEX.

188 MI.

276 MILES

Gila R.

MORMON

Arkansas
R.

YUMA

TUCSON

626 MILES

Pacific
Ocean

A MILITARY MARCH OVER 2000 MILES

"History may be searched in vain for an equal march of infantry
. . . through a wilderness of savages and wild beasts . . . or
deserts with no water . . . marching half naked and half fed we
have discovered and made a road of great value for our
country . . ."

Colonel St. George Cooke
San Diego, California
January 30, 1847

Grande
R.

Gulf of
Mexico

THE MARCH OF THE
MORMON BATTALION
(July 20, 1846  —  Jan. 29, 1847)

MEXICO

THE INDIANS were a constant threat to the Pioneers. At night the wagons were brought into a circle, and the horses and mules were tied inside the circle of wagons, while the oxen and cattle were guarded a safe distance from camp.

When the Pioneers camped by a stream they formed a semicircle with the wagons, the river forming one side of their defense. One of the front wheels of each wagon was rolled against the hind wheel of the wagon ahead. Most of the men took turns standing guard over the cattle at night.

Swift streams had to be crossed. There were always hazards to meet. As they met and overcame them they would leave behind trails and rafts as well as instructions to help those who would follow.

After the long trek of the day, with its chores done and the meal over, they would often sing and dance to divert their thoughts from the devious tasks of the day and the sorrows of parting from loved ones who had died on the way and were buried along the trail.

**WAGON CIRCLE**                    **by William H. Jackson**

## COME, COME, YE SAINTS

Come, come, ye Saints, no toil nor labor fear;
   But with joy wend your way.
Tho' hard to you this journey may appear,
   Grace shall be as your day.
'Tis better far for us to strive
   Our useless cares from us to drive;
Do this, and joy your hearts will swell —
   All is well! All is well!

Why should we mourn, or think our lot is hard?
   'Tis not so; all is right.
Why should we think to earn a great reward,
   If we now shun the fight?
Gird up your loins; fresh courage take;
   Our God will never us forsake;
And soon we'll have this tale to tell —
   All is well! All is well!

We'll find the place which God for us prepared,
   Far away in the West;
Where none shall come to hurt or make afraid;
   There the Saints will be blessed.
We'll make the air with music ring,
   Shout praises to our God and King;
Above the rest these words we'll tell —
   All is well! All is well!

And should we die before our journey's through,
   Happy day! all is well!
We then are free from toil and sorrow, too;
   With the just we shall dwell!
But if our lives are spared again
   To see the Saints their rest obtain,
O how we'll make this chorus swell —
   All is well! All is well!

**Written by William Clayton in April, 1846, to cheer the Pioneers as they crossed the plains.**

## O MY FATHER

O my Father, thou that dwellest
   In the high and glorious place!
When shall I regain thy presence
   And again behold thy face?
In thy holy habitation
   Did my spirit once reside?
In my first primeval childhood
   Was I nurtured near thy side ?

For a wise and glorious purpose
   Thou hast placed me here on earth
And withheld the recollection
   Of my former friends and birth;
Yet oft-times a secret something
   Whispered, ''You're a stranger here'';
And I felt that I had wandered
   From a more exalted sphere.

I had learned to call thee, Father,
   Through thy Spirit from on high;
But, until the Key of Knowledge
   Was restored, I knew not why.
In the heavens are parents single?
   No; the thought makes reason stare!
Truth is reason; truth eternal
   Tells me I've a mother there.

When I leave this frail existence,
   When I lay this mortal by,
Father, Mother, may I meet you
   In your royal courts on high?
Then, at length, when I've completed
   All you sent me forth to do,
With your mutual approbation
   Let me come and dwell with you.

**Written by Eliza R. Snow in 1843. It is a doctrinal hymn portraying the Mormon belief in man's relationship to God and in the literalness of the resurrection.**

ON AUGUST 6, 1842, Joseph Smith made the following prophecy: "I prophesied that the Saints would continue to suffer much affliction and would be driven to the Rocky Mountains, many would appostatize, others would be put to death by our persecutors, or lose their lives in consequence of exposure or disease, and some of them would live to go and assist in making settlements and build cities and see the Saints become a mighty people in the midst of the Rocky Mountains."

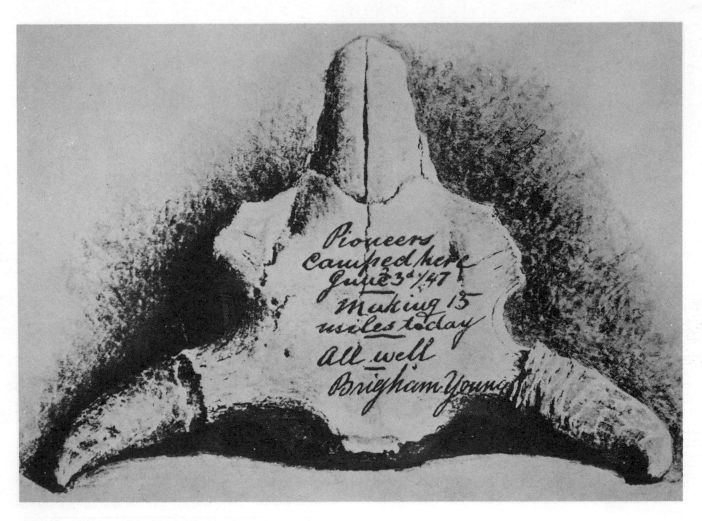

*Pioneers camped here June 3d/47 making 13 miles today All well Brigham Young*

**THE BULLETIN OF THE PLAINS**

THE FIRST, or vanguard, Pioneer company that started from Winter Quarters on April 7, 1847, on its trail-blazing and historic trek westward to the valley of the Great Salt Lake included a select group of men. Among them were most of the leaders of the Church. A total of one hundred forty-three picked men, three women and two children made up this first group to leave the headquarters on the banks of the Missouri River.

On June 1, 1847, which marked Brigham Young's 46th birthday, this advance group arrived at Fort Laramie. They had traveled 541 miles from Winter Quarters during a trek of seven weeks. Here at Fort Laramie they met

members of the "Mississippi Mormons" who had spent the winter at Pueblo, having come from the Southern States to join the Pioneers on the trail to the Great Salt Lake Valley. This addition to the vanguard group increased its number to 161. On June 21 they arrived at Independence Rock (now in western Wyoming), and then at South Pass, the famous "gateway to the West," on June 27th. A little farther on they met James Bridger, trapper and mountaineer, who was on his way to Fort Laramie.

After Brigham Young and the other leaders had expressed their intention of locating in the Great Salt Lake Valley, Bridger said he would give one thousand dollars for a bushel of corn raised in the Great Basin.

**COMING THROUGH THE MOUNTAINS**　　　　　　　　　　　　　　**by G. M. Ottinger**

THE TREK across the plains and mountains made by the Pioneers was organized in a military order. While on the march the wagons were kept close together and every man was required to ride or walk beside his own wagon and not to leave it without permission.

Brigham Young had issued the following order:

"At five o'clock in the morning the bugle is to be sounded as a signal for every man to rise and attend prayers before he leaves his wagon. Then the people will engage in cooking, eating, feeding teams, etc. until seven o'clock, at which time the train is to move at the sound of the bugle. Each teamster is to keep beside his team with loaded gun in hand or within easy reach, while the extra men, observing the same rule regarding their weapons, are to walk by the side of the particular wagons to which they belong; and no man may leave his post without the permission of the officers. In case of an attack or any hostile demonstration by Indians, the wagons will travel in double file — the order of encampment to be in a circle, with the mouth of each wagon to be outside, and the horses and cattle tied inside the circle. At half past eight each evening the bugles are to be sounded again, upon which signal all will hold prayers in their wagons, and be retired to rest by nine o'clock."

Copyright 1957 by Glenn E. Nielson,
In trust for the Cody Ward Mural Trust

The barren and bleak Salt Lake Valley as first seen by the Pioneers.　　　by H. L. A. Culmer

The last leg of the journey as the Pioneers entered Salt Lake Valley.　　　by J. Leo Fairbanks

Many of the pioneers would have gladly gone on to California or to the Northwest Territory, but when their inspired leader Brigham Young, on viewing the desolate valley of the Great Salt Lake on the 24th of July, 1847, said, "This is the place," that decided it for all. From a painting by Edward Grigware.

Copyright 1957 by Glenn E. Nielson,
Trustee in trust for the Cody Ward Mural Trust

**DELIVERANCE BY SEA GULLS**                                    by Edward Grigware

## THE CRICKETS' PLAGUE AND DELIVERANCE

T HE MORMON PIONEERS arrived in the Salt Lake Valley on July 24, 1847. Almost immediately they began clearing and plowing the ground. The first winter was mild,

and they were able to plant more than five thousand acres. Much of this was planted with winter wheat.

In the following spring, when the green grain started to grow, myriads of large crickets swarmed down on the growing crops to devour them. The Pioneers tried every means they had to destroy the crickets, without success. In final desperation they pleaded in prayer to the Lord to save the life-giving crops. Then, to their astonishment, they saw great flocks of sea gulls fly onto the fields and de-vour the crickets. The birds flew away, disgorged the crickets, and returned to repeat the process until the crops were saved.

## SEA GULLS CAME TO THE RESCUE

In commemoration of this great life-saving event, a fitting monument to the sea gull has been erected on Temple Square (above), which bears the inscription, "Erected in Grateful Remembrance of the Mercy of God to the Mormon Pioneers." A state law now prohibits the killing of the sea gull which is the State bird.

## MORMON HANDCART FAMILY

by Torleif Knaphus

ON SEPTEMBER 30, 1855, President Brigham Young announced the plan of walking across the prairies with handcarts:

". . . We cannot afford to purchase wagons and teams as in times past. I am consequently thrown back upon my old plan — to make handcarts and let the emigration foot it, and draw upon them the necessary supplies, having a cow or two for every ten. They can come just as quick if not quicker, and much cheaper — can start earlier and escape the prevailing sickness which annually lays so many of our brethren in the dust. A great majority of them walk now even with the teams which are provided, and have a great deal more care and perplexity than they would have if they came without them. They will only need ninety days ration from the time of their leaving the Missouri River and as the settlements extend up the Platte, not that much. The carts can be made without a particle of iron, with wheels hooped, made strong and light, and one, or if the family be large, two of them will bring all that they will need upon the plains.

". . . a company of this kind should make the trip in sixty or seventy days. I do know that they can beat any ox train crossing the plains."

"Let all the Saints who can . . . come while the way is open before them; let the poor also come; . . . let them come on foot, with handcarts, or wheelbarrows; let them gird up their loins and walk through, and nothing shall hinder or stay them."

To each hundred were alloted five tents, twenty handcarts, and one wagon drawn by three yoke of oxen. Tents and general supplies were stowed in the wagons, but each family carried its own rations and its quota of the sick and helpless in the handcart, while the women and children, from the toddlers to the aged, walked the weary trail from Winter Quarters on the Missouri River to the valley of the Great Salt Lake.

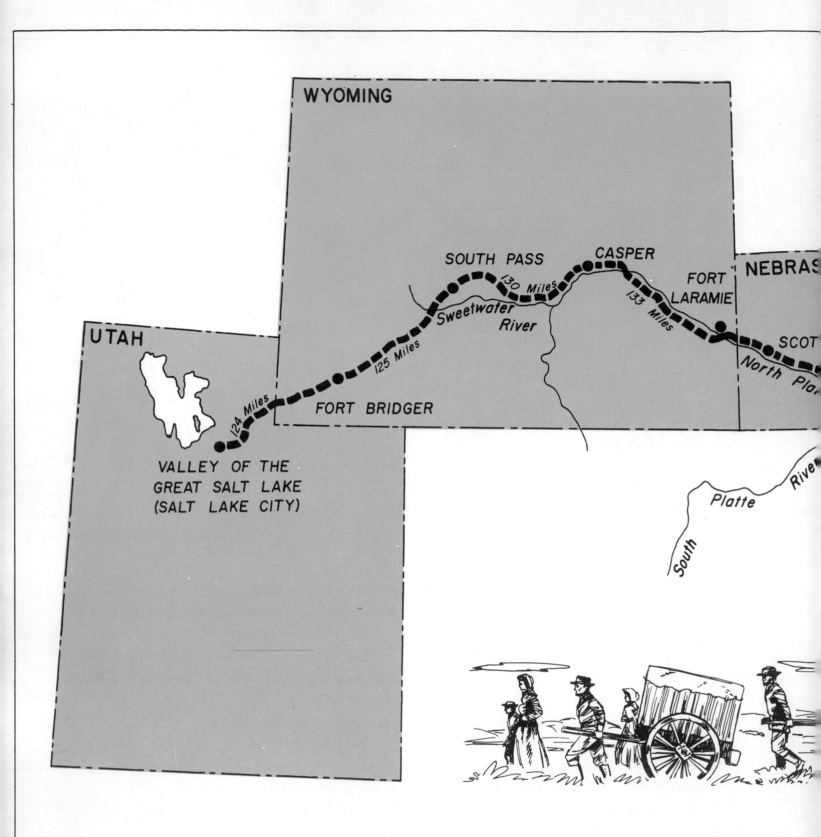

# THE ROUTE
## OF THE
# MORMON HANDCART PIONEERS
## (1856 — 1860)

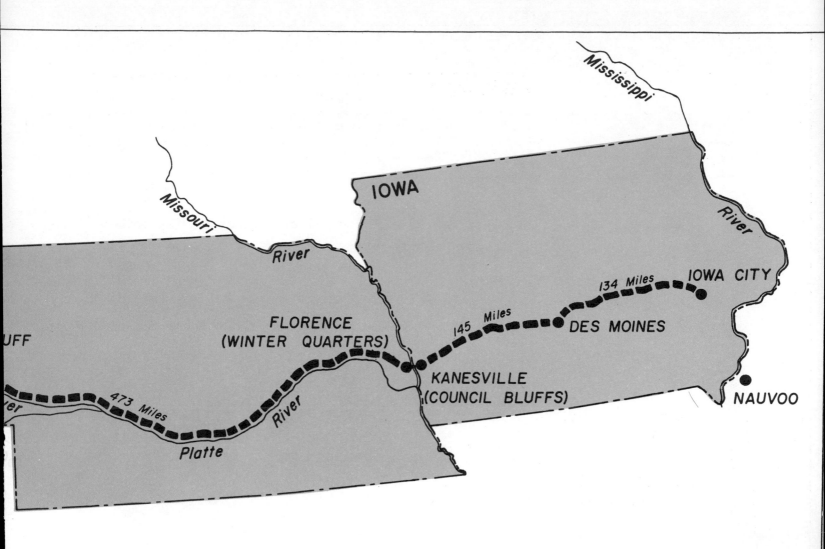

IOWA

Mississippi

Missouri

River

River

IOWA CITY

134 Miles

145 Miles

DES MOINES

FLORENCE
(WINTER QUARTERS)

KANESVILLE
(COUNCIL BLUFFS)

NAUVOO

473 Miles

River

Platte

UFF

er

Over 3,000 people came to the valley of the Great Salt Lake in handcart companies. From Iowa City, they treked over 1,300 miles, and averaged 85 days for the entire journey.

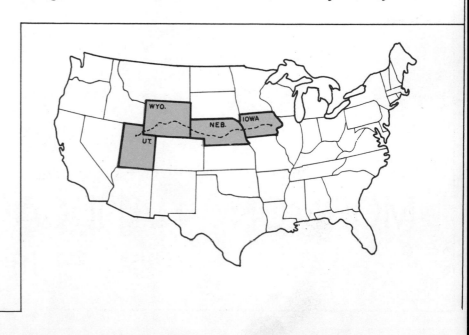

## THOSE WHO FOLLOWED . . .

TO ASSIST the thousands of converts coming daily from Europe a Perpetual Emigration Fund Company was organized in 1849, just two years after the first group of Pioneers, headed by Brigham Young, arrived in the Great Salt Lake Valley. For a period of nearly thirty years thereafter this program helped over forty thousand emigrants get to Utah.

Two of the handcart companies suffered greatly. They had been delayed in their departure from Iowa City. The authorities in Salt Lake City had not been informed of their coming. A marker near South Pass, Wyoming, describes the tragedy. Of the company of 404 persons, 77 perished before help arrived.

As soon as word reached Salt Lake City, help was rushed to them even at great risk, because of the heavy snow. The survivors reached Salt Lake City November 9, 1856.

**Friendly Indians helped in many ways. . . .**

These two pictures show typical pioneer wagon trains that went east from Salt Lake City to the terminal of the railroad to meet the immigrants and bring them to Salt Lake Valley.

**PIONEER WAGONS**                                          **by William H. Jackson**

THE PONY EXPRESS brought valuable information regarding Mormon emigrant trains coming west. It helped in a critical time to carry dispatches from Salt Lake City headquarters to Mormons living in the middle west and eastern parts of the country.

Although it operated for only 16 months (1860-1861) before the transcontinental telegraph was completed, the Pony Express performed a very valuable service.

The "Line" had 190 stations, 400 station-men assistants and 80 riders. Each rider rode from 100 to 140 miles at breakneck speed, with relays of horses at distances of from 20 to 25 miles. Rain, hail, snow, sleet or hostile

Indians — there was no delay night or day over the nearly 2000 miles from St. Joseph, Missouri, to Sacramento, California, via Salt Lake City, Utah.

The first rider left St. Joseph, Missouri, on April 3, 1860, headed west, and almost simultaneously another rider galloped out of Sacramento, California, eastward bound. The last westbound rider arrived in Sacramento 9 days and 23 hours after the first rider had departed from St. Joseph. The run had broken all previous records by 11 days. The last eastbound rider arrived in St. Joseph in 11 days and 12 hours. The mail rate for letters was $5.00 for each one-half ounce.

# EXPRESS

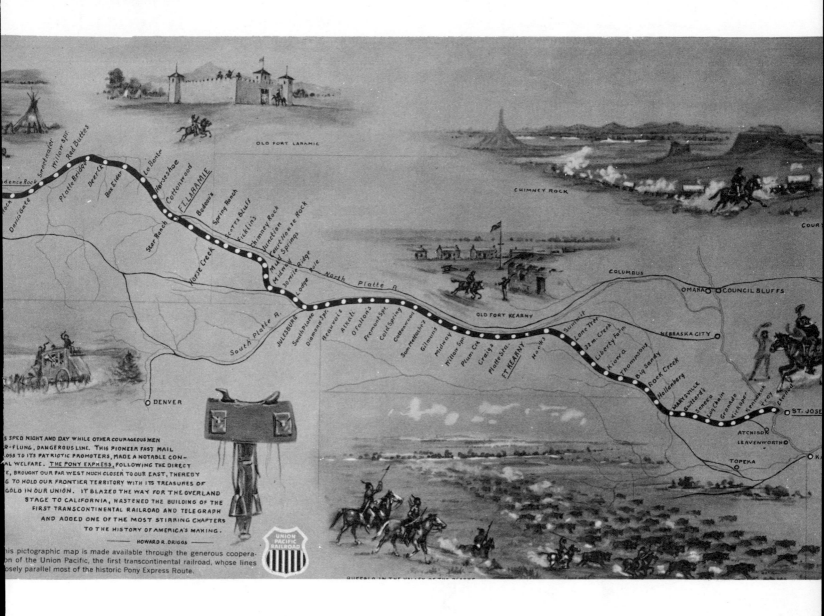

...S SPED NIGHT AND DAY WHILE OTHER COURAGEOUS MEN
...R-FLUNG, DANGEROUS LINE. THIS PIONEER FAST MAIL
...OSS TO ITS PATRIOTIC PROMOTERS, MADE A NOTABLE CON-
...AL WELFARE. THE PONY EXPRESS, FOLLOWING THE DIRECT
...E, BROUGHT OUR FAR WEST MUCH CLOSER TO OUR EAST, THEREBY
...G TO HOLD OUR FRONTIER TERRITORY WITH ITS TREASURES OF
...GOLD IN OUR UNION. IT BLAZED THE WAY FOR THE OVERLAND
STAGE TO CALIFORNIA, HASTENED THE BUILDING OF THE
FIRST TRANSCONTINENTAL RAILROAD AND TELEGRAPH
AND ADDED ONE OF THE MOST STIRRING CHAPTERS
TO THE HISTORY OF AMERICA'S MAKING.

—— HOWARD R. DRIGGS ——

...his pictographic map is made available through the generous coopera-
...n of the Union Pacific, the first transcontinental railroad, whose lines
...osely parallel most of the historic Pony Express Route.

**The Pony Express
The Change of Horses at the Post
by Avard Fairbanks**

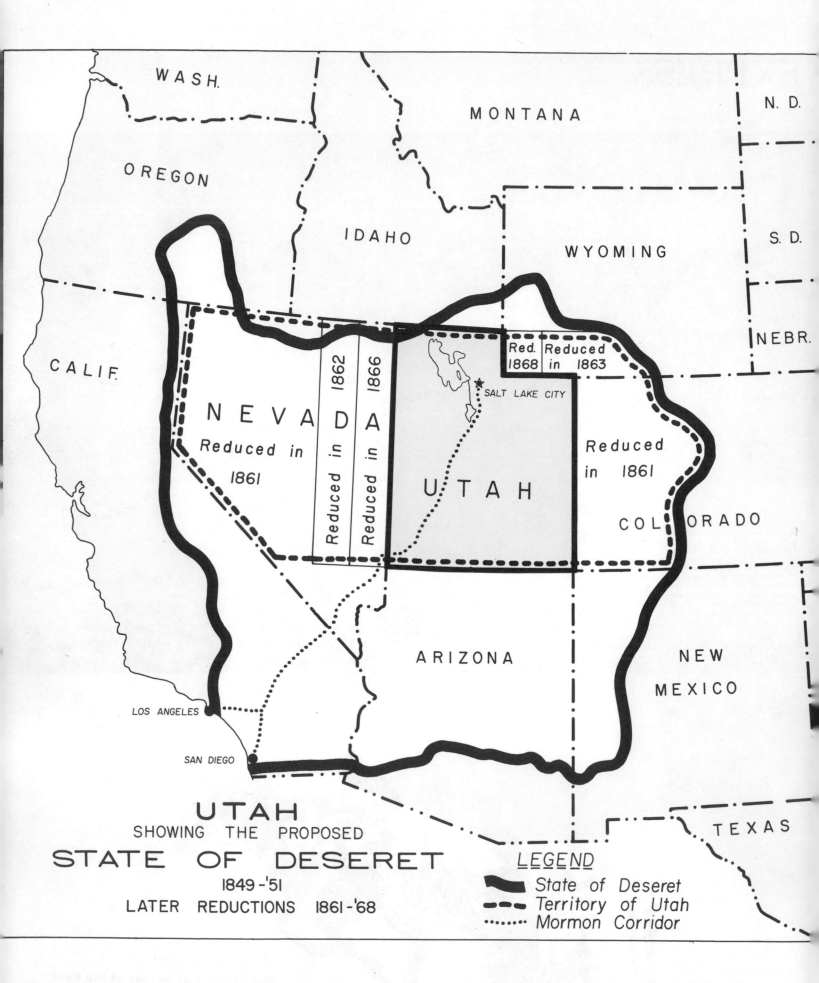

WASH.
MONTANA
N. D.
OREGON
IDAHO
WYOMING
S. D.
NEBR.
CALIF.
NEVADA
Reduced in
1861
Reduced in 1862
Reduced in 1866
Red. 1868
Reduced in 1863
UTAH
SALT LAKE CITY
Reduced in 1861
COLORADO
ARIZONA
NEW MEXICO
LOS ANGELES
SAN DIEGO
TEXAS

UTAH
SHOWING THE PROPOSED
STATE OF DESERET
1849-'51
LATER REDUCTIONS 1861-'68

LEGEND
State of Deseret
Territory of Utah
Mormon Corridor

**The map shows the outline of the Provisional State of Deseret as adopted by the Constitutional Convention which met in Salt Lake City, March 10, 1849. Map also shows how the territory of Deseret was "whittled" down and the name changed to the UTAH TERRITORY in 1851, then to the present STATE OF UTAH in 1896.**

# The Mormon State of Deseret

WITH THE rapid expansion of the United States, problems of government and supervision arose in the newly-acquired territories. The Federal Government had failed to provide any form of government for the inhabitants of the Great Basin territory. The Mormons followed what had been previously done by pioneering groups in other areas, such as Tennessee, North Carolina, Oregon, and California, and that was to create some form of government among themselves for order, protection and progress.

The flow of immigrants was increasing. The new "Gospel" philosophy that the Mormon missionaries were sharing with peoples all over oppressed Europe was taking hold. Many fertile places had to be found to make homes for the large influx of converts.

In March of 1849, the State of "Deseret" (the name "Deseret" taken from the Book of Mormon, meaning "Honey Bee") was organized among the Mormons, with an area that included all of what is now Utah, Nevada, most of Arizona, parts of Idaho, Oregon, Colorado, New Mexico and California. The California part included San Diego and north along the coast to Los Angeles.

Brigham Young planned to include a seaport (San Diego) in the State of Deseret so that a "corridor" from that port to the Great Salt Lake Basin could be made. This would help the emigrants from the Eastern states and from Europe who came to the west coast by ship after crossing the Isthmus of Panama or going around South America. Coming this way, the Mormon emigrants would have less difficulty and be free from the long and tedious trek across the Indian-infested plains and also would avoid the unfriendly white settlements. A string of Mormon settlements was planned from San Diego to Salt Lake where emigrants could stop enroute and receive friendly hospitality.

On September 9, 1850, Congress designated this area as the "Utah Territory" and reduced its size from the Mormon State of Deseret to that shown on the map (opposite page). Congress also changed the Mormon name of Deseret to Utah, and President Millard Fillmore appointed Brigham Young as Governor of the newly-formed territory.

The long delay in granting statehood to Utah was perhaps at first due to the Southerners, who, in control of Congress, feared that Utah would, if admitted, come in as a "free" state and not as a slave state. Then after the Civil War, the question of polygamy postponed the recognition until 1896, when the Territory of Utah was reduced and became a state in its present size.

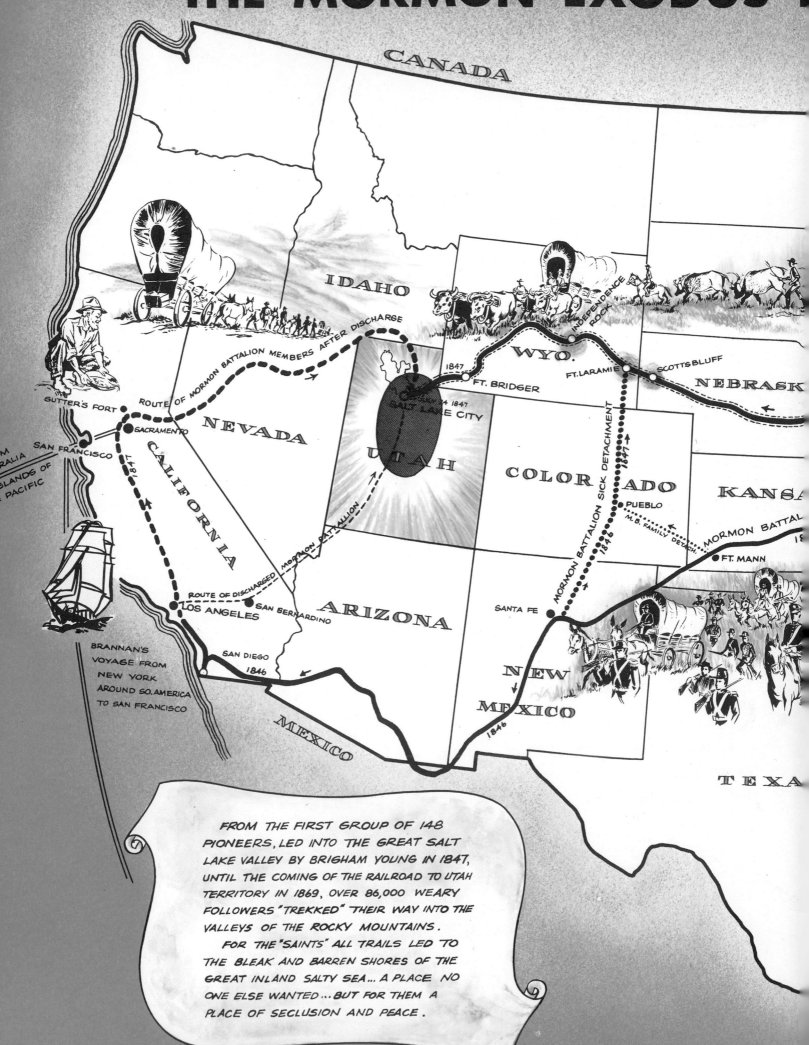

FROM THE FIRST GROUP OF 148
PIONEERS, LED INTO THE GREAT SALT
LAKE VALLEY BY BRIGHAM YOUNG IN 1847,
UNTIL THE COMING OF THE RAILROAD TO UTAH
TERRITORY IN 1869, OVER 86,000 WEARY
FOLLOWERS "TREKKED" THEIR WAY INTO THE
VALLEYS OF THE ROCKY MOUNTAINS.
FOR THE "SAINTS" ALL TRAILS LED TO
THE BLEAK AND BARREN SHORES OF THE
GREAT INLAND SALTY SEA... A PLACE NO
ONE ELSE WANTED... BUT FOR THEM A
PLACE OF SECLUSION AND PEACE.

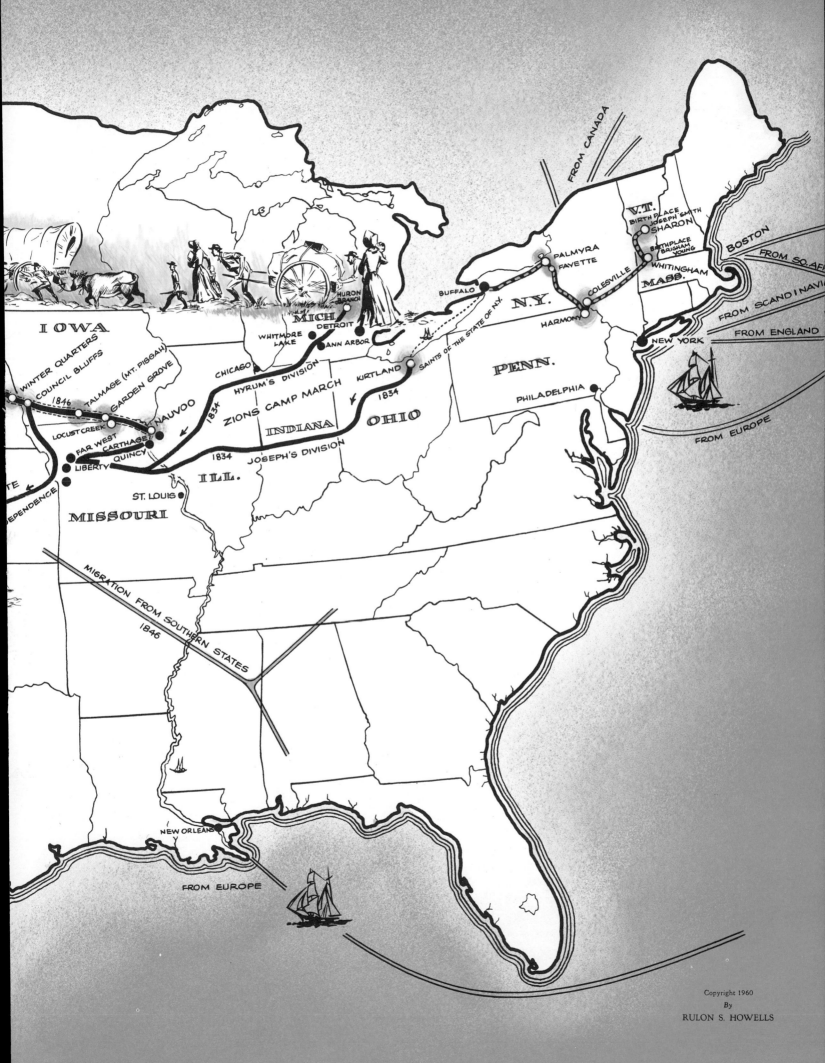

# THE ROCKY MOUNTAINS

FROM CANADA

V.T.
BIRTH PLACE
JOSEPH SMITH
SHARON

BIRTHPLACE
BRIGHAM
YOUNG

BOSTON

PALMYRA
FAYETTE

WHITINGHAM

FROM SO. AF

COLESVILLE

MASS.

FROM SCANDINAVI

BUFFALO

N.Y.

FROM ENGLAND

HARMONY

HURON
BRANCH

SAINTS OF THE STATE OF N.Y.

NEW YORK

MICH.
DETROIT

WHITMORE
LAKE

ANN ARBOR

KIRTLAND

PENN.

IOWA

CHICAGO

HYRUM'S DIVISION

1834

PHILADELPHIA

FROM EUROPE

WINTER QUARTERS
COUNCIL BLUFFS

TALMAGE (MT. PISGAH)
GARDEN GROVE

1846

LOCUST CREEK

FAR WEST
CARTHAGE
QUINCY

LIBERTY

NAUVOO

1834

ZIONS CAMP MARCH

1834

INDIANA

OHIO

JOSEPH'S DIVISION

ILL.

DEPENDENCE

ST. LOUIS

MISSOURI

MIGRATION FROM SOUTHERN STATES

1846

NEW ORLEANS

FROM EUROPE

Copyright 1960
By
RULON S. HOWELLS

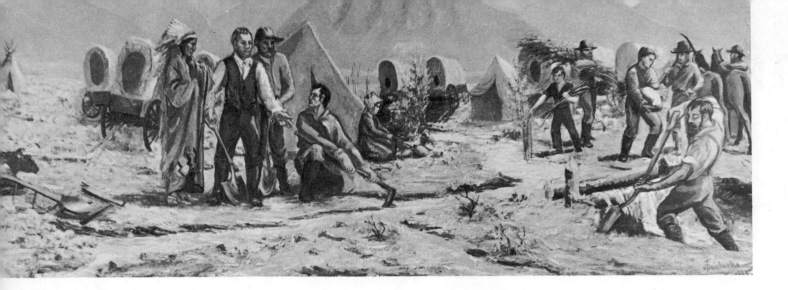

Just a few hours after the arrival of the first Pioneers in the Salt Lake Valley, in July, 1847, they tried to plow the ground preparatory to planting potatoes. The ground was so hard and dry they broke the plows. They then diverted the water from one of the near-by canyon streams and soaked the soil; it was then easier to plow. This and subsequent waterings marked the beginning of modern irrigation practice in America. Above picture is by J. B. Fairbanks.

Early Salt Lake City showing the Tabernacle completed and the Temple about one and a half stories high. Taken in 1883. Looking down Main Street from about First North Street.

Salt Lake City from Main Street looking east on South Temple Street, showing Brigham's residences — the Lion House and the Beehive House.

One of the earliest pictures of Salt Lake City. Looking down Main Street from about First North Street.

G. S. L. City. Jan. 20. 1849.

No

GOOD to N. K. Whitney

one DOLLAR on demand.

B. Young

H. C. Kimball

T. Bullock Clerk.

$1.00d

$.00d

or bearer.

The Mormon Pioneers, out of necessity for a medium of exchange, printed much of their own currency.

Freighting "Trains" that hauled the Pioneers and their provisions from the end of the railroad to Salt Lake Valley.

## THEY KEPT COMING . . . . . . . .

LARGE NUMBERS of teams were sent from Salt Lake City each season to meet the immigrants at the western terminus of the railroad. As the railroad advanced westward the overland trip by wagon from and to Salt Lake City was shortened.

During the period from 1861 to 1868 there were approximately 2,400 men employed with

In the winter snow, mud and cold,

in the summer dust and thirst . . .

about 2,000 wagons and nearly 18,000 oxen to meet the trains carrying immigrants.

The largest single wagon train of Mormons coming to Utah was in 1866, with 500 persons, 456 teamsters, 3,042 oxen, 397 wagons, 89 horses and 134 mules.

**CULTURE IN THE WILDERNESS —** ⇧

Cornelius Salisbury

The Social Hall Theatre, built in 1852, just five years after the first Pioneers entered the Salt Lake Valley. Seating capacity 300. Used for theatrical events, banquets, and dancing.

The Salt Lake Theatre, built in 1861. A really remarkable building. Brigham Young said when its construction was started, "The people ⇩ must have amusement as well as religion."

Early photo of Salt Lake City showing the foundation of the Temple and the completed Tabernacle.

Salt Lake City Main Street between South Temple and Third South Streets. About 1880.

THIS WAS a place of seclusion their inspired leader Brigham Young was seeking. From their beginning in New York State, the Mormons had known only persecution from those among whom they had made their settlements, but here in these barren waste lands, with only Indians as neighbors, they had peace and contentment.

The tranquility and seclusion the Mormons finally found was graphically described at the time by Parley P. Pratt, a Mormon poet and writer, in a letter to his brother, Orson Pratt, who was in England in 1848: "I have now resided almost one year in this lone retreat where civilized man has not made his home for the last thousand years, and where the ripening harvest has not been enjoyed for ages until this present season.

"During all this period, the sound of war, the rise and fall of empires, the revolution of states and kingdoms — news of any kind has scarcely reached my ears. It is but a few days since we heard of the revolutions and convulsions which are agitating Europe. All is quiet — stillness. No elections, no police reports, no murders, no wars, in our little world. How quiet, how still, how peaceful, how happy, how lonesome, how free from excitement we live. The legislation of our High Council, the decision of some judge or court of the Church, a meeting, a dance, a visit, an exploring tour, an arrival of a party of trappers and traders, a Mexican caravan, a party arrived from the Pacific, from the States, from Fort Hall or Fort Bridger; a visit of an Indian perhaps, a mail from the distant world once or twice a year, is all that breaks up the monotony of our busy and peaceful life. Our old firelocks have not been rubbed up or our swords unsheathed because of any alarm.

"No policemen or watchmen of any kind have been on duty to guard us from external or internal danger. Oh! what a life we live! It is the dream of the poets actually fulfilled."

**Salt Lake City, looking east from Main Street along South Temple Street. The Hotel Utah corner lower left. The steel framework of the Deseret Gymnasium left center. The Zion's Savings Bank building then recently finished on the right. (Photo about 1910)**

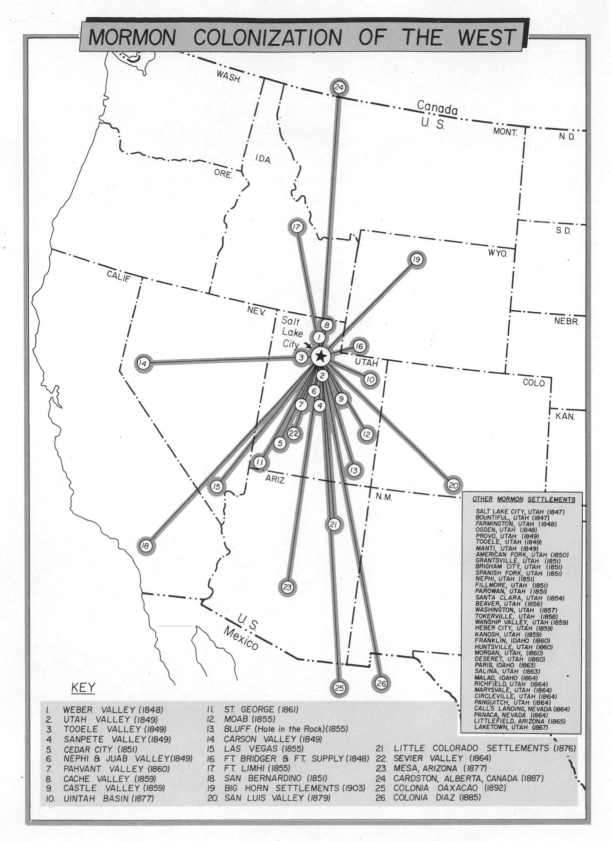

**KEY**

| | |
|---|---|
| 1. WEBER VALLEY (1848) | 11. ST. GEORGE (1861) |
| 2. UTAH VALLEY (1849) | 12. MOAB (1855) |
| 3. TOOELE VALLEY (1849) | 13. BLUFF (Hole in the Rock) (1855) |
| 4. SANPETE VALLEY (1849) | 14. CARSON VALLEY (1849) |
| 5. CEDAR CITY (1851) | 15. LAS VEGAS (1855) |
| 6. NEPHI & JUAB VALLEY (1849) | 16. FT. BRIDGER & FT. SUPPLY (1848) |
| 7. PAHVANT VALLEY (1860) | 17. FT. LIMHI (1855) |
| 8. CACHE VALLEY (1859) | 18. SAN BERNARDINO (1851) |
| 9. CASTLE VALLEY (1859) | 19. BIG HORN SETTLEMENTS (1903) |
| 10. UINTAH BASIN (1877) | 20. SAN LUIS VALLEY (1879) |

| | |
|---|---|
| 21. LITTLE COLORADO SETTLEMENTS (1876) |
| 22. SEVIER VALLEY (1864) |
| 23. MESA, ARIZONA (1877) |
| 24. CARDSTON, ALBERTA, CANADA (1887) |
| 25. COLONIA OAXACAO (1892) |
| 26. COLONIA DIAZ (1885) |

**OTHER MORMON SETTLEMENTS**

SALT LAKE CITY, UTAH (1847)
BOUNTIFUL, UTAH (1847)
FARMINGTON, UTAH (1848)
OGDEN, UTAH (1848)
PROVO, UTAH (1849)
TOOELE, UTAH (1849)
MANTI, UTAH (1849)
AMERICAN FORK, UTAH (1850)
GRANTSVILLE, UTAH (1851)
BRIGHAM CITY, UTAH (1851)
SPANISH FORK, UTAH (1851)
NEPHI, UTAH (1851)
FILLMORE, UTAH (1851)
PAROWAN, UTAH (1851)
SANTA CLARA, UTAH (1854)
BEAVER, UTAH (1856)
WASHINGTON, UTAH (1857)
TOKERVILLE, UTAH (1858)
WANSHIP VALLEY, UTAH (1859)
HEBER CITY, UTAH (1859)
KANOSH, UTAH (1859)
FRANKLIN, IDAHO (1860)
HUNTSVILLE, UTAH (1860)
MORGAN, UTAH (1860)
DESERET, UTAH (1860)
PARIS, IDAHO (1863)
SALINA, UTAH (1863)
MALAD, IDAHO (1864)
RICHFIELD, UTAH (1864)
MARYSVALE, UTAH (1864)
CIRCLEVILLE, UTAH (1864)
PANGUITCH, UTAH (1864)
CALL'S LANDING, NEVADA (1864)
PANACA, NEVADA (1864)
LITTLEFIELD, ARIZONA (1865)
LAKETOWN, UTAH (1867)

# Colonization of the Rocky Mountain Area and Adjoining Territories

**B**RIGHAM YOUNG called groups of people to move into various regions to settle and develop them. The purpose was to have the Mormons occupy most of the fertile valleys in the Rocky Mountains and adjoining areas. It was necessary to provide places to live for the stream of convert immigrants coming from Europe, and to have the surrounding territory occupied by friendly people.

One such group migrated from central to southeastern Utah and went through terrain so rugged that wagons had to be taken apart and transported piece by piece in some places, and in others let down by ropes, as in this picture on the opposite page by Farrell R. Collett of the "Hole in the Rock" group who settled the fertile valleys of Southeastern Utah.

74

# THE END OF ISOLATION . . .

Painting of Leland Stanford driving Golden Spike.        Union Pacific Depot, Salt Lake City, Utah

## ON MAY 10, 1869

The Central Pacific (now Southern Pacific) Railroad met the Union Pacific Railroad at Promontory, Utah. This picture was taken at the ceremony when the Golden Spike was driven and the continent spanned by steel.

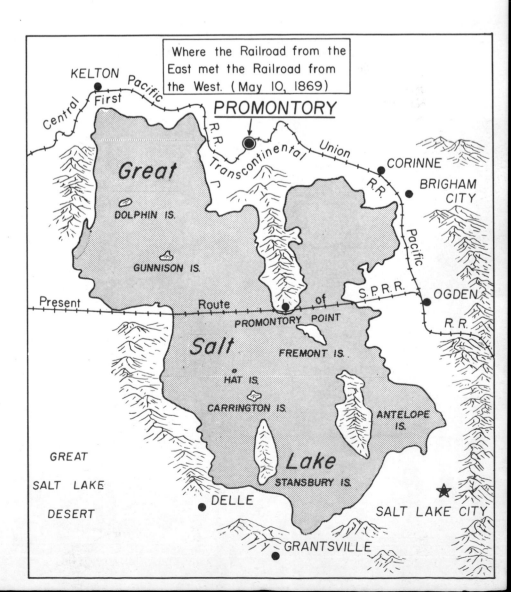

Where the Railroad from the East met the Railroad from the West. (May 10, 1869)

PROMONTORY

KELTON

CORINNE

BRIGHAM CITY

OGDEN

Great

DOLPHIN IS.

GUNNISON IS.

Present        Route        of

PROMONTORY POINT

Salt        FREMONT IS.

HAT IS.

CARRINGTON IS.

ANTELOPE IS.

Lake

STANSBURY IS.

GREAT SALT LAKE DESERT

DELLE

SALT LAKE CITY

GRANTSVILLE

# A Temple In the Wilderness

**THE SALT LAKE TEMPLE IN CONSTRUCTION**
Picture below shows an insert of how Pioneers
hand-cut the huge granite stones. Portrayed
by Edward Grigware.

**GRANITE QUARRY FOR THE SALT LAKE TEMPLE**
Above picture shows quarry located in Little
Cottonwood Canyon. By George R. Dunphy.

Copyright 1957 by Glenn E. Nielson, Trustee in trust for the Cody Ward Mural Trust

## THE SALT LAKE TEMPLE . . .

Started in 1853 and completed forty years later in 1893. Built of granite blocks hauled by oxen 20 miles from the Temple site. During its construction the desert around it was still being subdued and Indians were a constant threat.

# Why the Mormons Build Temples . . .

THE TEMPLES of the Church of Jesus Christ of Latter-day Saints are built for particular sacred ordinances. These ordinances are not secret to the thousands who perform them every day, but they are sacred.

The ceremonies performed in the Temples by all members of good standing in the Church pertain to the salvation of all peoples who have died without a knowledge of the full Gospel of Jesus Christ. These ceremonies are based upon the belief that the soul of every person born into this life from the very beginning of time will, after death, yet live as an individual in a tangible resurrected state and go on toward perfection.

It is for universal salvation of all mankind who accept the full Gospel of Jesus Christ that the ordinances and ceremonies are performed in the Temples by the living members for themselves first and then as proxies for those that have passed from this life into the next. This is not to be interpreted as any form of reincarnation, a doctrine in which the Mormons do not believe. Their belief is that all mankind has the privilege of eternal progression from this "grade" of life to another, with each individual retaining his or her identity, and with the family unit remaining intact.

The most illustrious example is that of Jesus Christ, who, after His resurrection, retained His identity and individuality. In like manner all mankind, i. e., each individual, will do this.

The words of Jesus to Nicodemus are accepted in their literal sense by the Mormons: "Except a man be born of the water and of the spirit, he cannot enter into the kingdom of God." (John 3:5)

If baptism is essential for one man, it is essential for all. Since our ancestors may never have heard of Jesus Christ nor had the opportunity to accept His teachings, they cannot be condemned. Thus Latter-day Saints believe in baptism for the dead. (I Corinthians 15:29; "Else what shall they do which are baptized for the dead, if the dead rise not at all? why are they then baptized for the dead?"

The Mormons believe that all mankind from the beginning may be saved by obedience to the laws and ordinances of the Gospel; that people who die without having been taught the Gospel may yet have the opportunity. This is made clear in the Scriptures, which make no distinction between the living and the dead. To provide a means of salvation for all, facilities are made available in the Temples whereby living proxies may be baptized in behalf of the deceased. (1 Peter 3:18-20; I Peter 4:6)

Celestial marriage is also an important rite within the Temples. When upon this earth, the Savior told His Apostles: "And I give unto thee the keys of the kingdom of heaven: and whatsoever thou shalt bind on earth shall be bound in heaven; and whatsoever thou shalt loose on earth shall be loosed in the heaven." (Matthew 16:19) The Mormons claim to have that same divine power of sealing.

When a marriage is performed in the Mormon Temples, the ordinance is sealed under the authority of the Holy (divine) Priesthood. The contracting parties are wed not only for this life or "until death do thee part," as is the case in civil and other church marriages, but with the Mormons the virtue of love continues and the couples are united for "time and eternity," or for this life and for the next life. The marriage covenant with its attendant obligations is made an everlasting contract. In the heavens the family relationship will continue. Nowhere other than in these sacred Temples is marriage for time and eternity performed. The bonds of love between husband and wife, and children and parents are made of eternal duration.

After a Temple is finished and prior to its official dedication, the general public is permitted to go throughout the building for viewing. A Temple is dedicated by ceremonies and prayer, after which it is used only for the specific purposes as above described.

**THE KIRTLAND TEMPLE,** Kirtland, Ohio, Dedicated March 27, 1836. (Not now owned nor used by the Church of Jesus Christ of Latter-day Saints.)

**THE NAUVOO TEMPLE,** Nauvoo, Illinois, Dedicated May 1, 1846. (Subsequently destroyed by fire.)

**THE ST. GEORGE TEMPLE**, St. George, Utah, Dedicated April 6, 1877.

**THE LOGAN TEMPLE**, Logan, Utah, Dedicated May 17, 1884.

**THE MANTI TEMPLE, Manti, Utah, Dedicated May 21, 1888.**

**THE SALT LAKE TEMPLE, Salt Lake City, Utah, Dedicated April 6, 1893.**

**THE HAWAIIAN TEMPLE,** Laie, Oahu, Hawaii, Dedicated November 27, 1919.

**THE CANADIAN TEMPLE,** Cardston, Alberta, Canada,

**Dedicated August 26, 1923.**

**THE ARIZONA TEMPLE**, Mesa, Arizona, Dedicated October 23, 1927.

**THE IDAHO FALLS TEMPLE**, Idaho Falls, Idaho,
Dedicated September 23, 1945.

**THE SWISS TEMPLE** ⇨
Bern, Switzerland
Dedicated September 11, 1955

**THE LOS ANGELES TEMPLE** ⇦
Los Angeles, California
Dedicated March 11, 1956

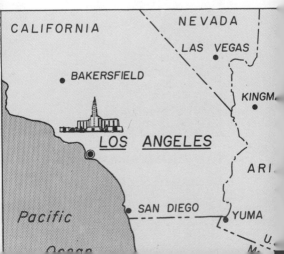

**THE BRITISH TEMPLE**
Newchapel, Surrey, England
Dedicated September 7, 1958

**THE NEW ZEALAND TEMPLE**
Near Hamilton, New Zealand
Dedicated April 20, 1958

# Where Did the Mormons Come From?

THE MORMONS have a different philosophy of life to share with the world. They dedicate their lives, their means and talents to promulgate this different concept of life to all non-Mormons, and they instill this enthusiasm into all converts.

From the very beginning (1830) of the Mormon Church, the correct and true name of which is **The Church of Jesus Christ of Latter-day Saints**, new converts were sent as missionaries to various states and abroad to England and the continent of Europe, as well as to the islands of the Pacific Ocean. Thousands of people of all classes joined the Church and were encouraged to migrate to the Rocky Mountains where they could form their own communities and live and build in peace.

Some of the choice people of European nations came as converts into the wilderness to establish new homes and take part in the reclamation of the American desert. It was truly a cosmopolitan society that "trekked" across the plains and into the Rocky Mountains to contribute to the agricultural, industrial, social and intellectual upbuilding of the new territory.

Many years before the Pioneers entered the Salt Lake Valley, Joseph Smith, the Prophet, founder and first President of the Church, prophesied "that the Saints would . . . be driven to the Rocky Mountains . . . and assist in making settlements and build cities . . . . and become a mighty people in the midst of the Rocky Mountains."

From 1847 to 1877 more than 70,000 European emigrant Mormons were brought into the Great Basin. They all traveled the last many hundreds of miles by horse or oxen-drawn wagons, or on foot, pulling a handcart with all their earthly possessions.

**The Mormon position among the Christian denominations of the world is unique. Mormons are not affiliated, either directly or indirectly, with any other Christian or non-Christian church or group.**

**The "Mormon" Church, or correctly speaking, The Church of Jesus Christ of Latter-day Saints, does not now have, nor has it ever had any connection or relation with any other church or religious group except the primitive Church, established by Jesus Christ nineteen centuries ago.**

**The chart on the opposite page attempts to show the position of the Mormon Church as to its distinct and separate origin—namely, that it was established through the personal visitation and by direct revelation of God the Father and Jesus Christ the Son to Joseph Smith in the spring of 1820. Numerous other revelations and visitations by heavenly personages came to Joseph Smith until the time of his death in 1844. Joseph Smith never belonged to any other church.**

**This chart also answers the questions frequently asked of the Mormons, "Are you Protestant or Catholic?"**

# APOSTACY AND RESTORATION

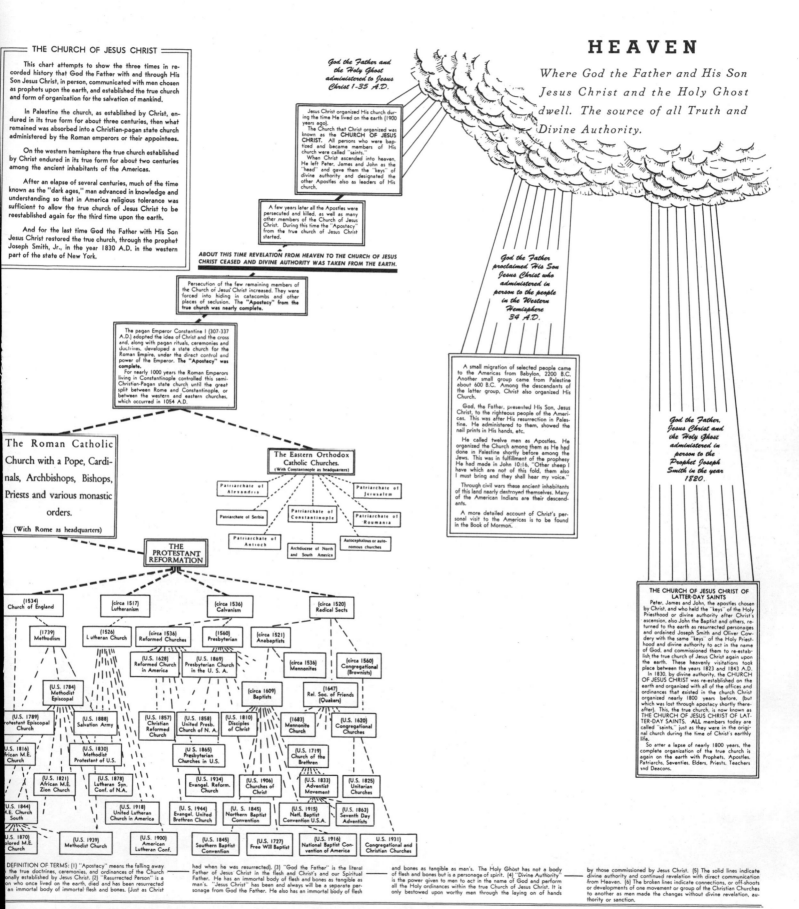

## THE CHURCH OF JESUS CHRIST

This chart attempts to show the three times in recorded history that God the Father with and through His Son Jesus Christ, in person, communicated with men chosen as prophets upon the earth, and established the true church and form of organization for the salvation of mankind.

In Palestine the church, as established by Christ, endured in its true form for about three centuries, then what remained was absorbed into a Christian-pagan state church administered by the Roman emperors or their appointees.

On the western hemisphere the true church established by Christ endured in its true form for about two centuries among the ancient inhabitants of the Americas.

After an elapse of several centuries, much of the time known as the "dark ages," man advanced in knowledge and understanding so that in America religious tolerance was sufficient to allow the true church of Jesus Christ to be reestablished again for the third time upon the earth.

And for the last time God the Father with His Son Jesus Christ restored the true church, through the prophet Joseph Smith, Jr., in the year 1830 A.D. in the western part of the state of New York.

## HEAVEN

*Where God the Father and His Son Jesus Christ and the Holy Ghost dwell. The source of all Truth and Divine Authority.*

*God the Father and the Holy Ghost administered to Jesus Christ 1-35 A.D.*

Jesus Christ organized His church during the time He lived on the earth (1900 years ago).
The Church that Christ organized was known as the CHURCH OF JESUS CHRIST. All persons who were baptized and became members of His church were called "saints."
When Christ ascended into heaven, He left Peter, James and John as the "head" and gave them the "keys" of divine authority and designated the other Apostles also as leaders of His church.

A few years later all the Apostles were persecuted and killed, as well as many other members of the Church of Jesus Christ. During this time the "Apostasy" from the true church of Jesus Christ started.

**ABOUT THIS TIME REVELATION FROM HEAVEN TO THE CHURCH OF JESUS CHRIST CEASED AND DIVINE AUTHORITY WAS TAKEN FROM THE EARTH.**

Persecution of the few remaining members of the Church of Jesus Christ increased. They were forced into hiding in catacombs and other places of seclusion. The "Apostasy" from the true church was nearly complete.

The pagan Emperor Constantine I (307-337 A.D.) adopted the idea of Christ and the cross and, along with pagan rituals, ceremonies and doctrines, developed a state church for the Roman Empire, under the direct control and power of the Emperor. The "Apostasy" was complete.
For nearly 1000 years the Roman Emperors living in Constantinople controlled this semi-Christian-Pagan state church until the great split between Rome and Constantinople, or between the western and eastern churches, which occurred in 1054 A.D.

*God the Father proclaimed His Son Jesus Christ who administered in person to the people in the Western Hemisphere 34 A.D.*

A small migration of selected people came to the Americas from Babylon, 2200 B.C. Another small group came from Palestine about 600 B.C. Among the descendants of the latter group, Christ also organized His Church.

God, the Father, presented His Son, Jesus Christ, to the righteous people of the Americas. This was after His resurrection in Palestine. He administered to them, showed the nail prints in His hands, etc.

He called twelve men as Apostles. He organized the Church among them as He had done in Palestine shortly before among the Jews. This was in fulfillment of the prophesy He had made in John 10:16, "Other sheep I have which are not of this fold, them also I must bring and they shall hear my voice."

Through civil wars these ancient inhabitants of this land nearly destroyed themselves. Many of the American Indians are their descendants.

A more detailed account of Christ's personal visit to the Americas is to be found in the Book of Mormon.

*God the Father, Jesus Christ and the Holy Ghost administered in person to the Prophet Joseph Smith in the year 1820.*

## The Roman Catholic

Church with a Pope, Cardinals, Archbishops, Bishops, Priests and various monastic orders.

(With Rome as headquarters)

### The Eastern Orthodox Catholic Churches.
(With Constantinople as headquarters)

- Patriarchate of Alexandria
- Patriarchate of Jerusalem
- Patriarchate of Serbia
- Patriarchate of Constantinople
- Patriarchate of Roumania
- Patriarchate of Antioch
- Archdiocese of North and South America
- Autocephalous or autonomous churches

### THE PROTESTANT REFORMATION

- (1534) Church of England
- (circa 1517) Lutheranism
- (circa 1536) Calvinism
- (circa 1520) Radical Sects
- (1739) Methodism
- (1526) Lutheran Church
- (circa 1536) Reformed Churches
- (1560) Presbyterian
- (circa 1521) Anabaptists
- (U.S. 1628) Reformed Church in America
- (U.S. 1869) Presbyterian Church in the U. S. A.
- (circa 1536) Mennonites
- (circa 1560) Congregational (Brownists)
- (U.S. 1784) Methodist Episcopal
- (circa 1609) Baptists
- (1647) Rel. Soc. of Friends (Quakers)
- (U.S. 1789) Protestant Episcopal Church
- (U.S. 1888) Salvation Army
- (U.S. 1857) Christian Reformed Church
- (U.S. 1858) United Presb. Church of N. A.
- (U.S. 1810) Disciples of Christ
- (1683) Mennonite Church
- (U.S. 1620) Congregational Churches
- (U.S. 1816) African M.E. Church
- (U.S. 1830) Methodist Protestant of U.S.
- (U.S. 1865) Presbyterian Churches in U.S.
- (U.S. 1719) Church of the Brethren
- (U.S. 1821) African M.E. Zion Church
- (U.S. 1878) Lutheran Syn. Conf. of N.A.
- (U.S. 1934) Evangel. Reform. Church
- (U.S. 1906) Churches of Christ
- (U.S. 1833) Adventist Movement
- (U.S. 1825) Unitarian Churches
- (U.S. 1844) M.E. Church South
- (U.S. 1918) United Lutheran Church in America
- (U.S. 1944) Evangel. United Brethren Church
- (U.S. 1845) Northern Baptist Convention
- (U.S. 1915) Natl. Baptist Convention U.S.A.
- (U.S. 1863) Seventh Day Adventists
- (U.S. 1870) Colored M.E. Church
- (U.S. 1939) Methodist Church
- (U.S. 1900) American Lutheran Conf.
- (U.S. 1845) Southern Baptist Convention
- (U.S. 1727) Free Will Baptist
- (U.S. 1916) National Baptist Convention of America
- (U.S. 1931) Congregational and Christian Churches

## THE CHURCH OF JESUS CHRIST OF LATTER-DAY SAINTS

Peter, James and John, the apostles chosen by Christ, and who held the "keys" of the Holy Priesthood or divine authority after Christ's ascension, also John the Baptist and others, returned to the earth as resurrected personages and ordained Joseph Smith and Oliver Cowdery with the same "keys" of the Holy Priesthood and divine authority to act in the name of God, and commissioned them to re-establish the true church of Jesus Christ again upon the earth. These heavenly visitations took place between the years 1823 and 1843 A.D.

In 1830, by divine authority, the CHURCH OF JESUS CHRIST was re-established on the earth and organized with all of the offices and ordinances that existed in the church Christ organized nearly 1800 years before, (but which was lost through apostacy shortly thereafter). This, the true church, is now known as THE CHURCH OF JESUS CHRIST OF LATTER-DAY SAINTS. ALL members today are called "saints," just as they were in the original church during the time of Christ's earthly life.

So after a lapse of nearly 1800 years, the complete organization of the true church is again on the earth with Prophets, Apostles, Patriarchs, Seventies, Elders, Priests, Teachers and Deacons.

---

**DEFINITION OF TERMS:** (1) "Apostasy" means the falling away from the true doctrines, ceremonies, and ordinances of the Church originally established by Jesus Christ. (2) "Resurrected Person" is a person who once lived on the earth, died and has been resurrected with an immortal body of immortal flesh and bones. (Just as Christ had when he was resurrected). (3) "God the Father" is the literal Father of Jesus Christ in the flesh and Christ's and our Spiritual Father. He has an immortal body of flesh and bones as tangible as man's. "Jesus Christ" has been and always will be a separate personage from God the Father. He also has an immortal body of flesh and bones as tangible as man's. The Holy Ghost has not a body of flesh and bones but is a personage of spirit. (4) "Divine Authority" is the power given to men to act in the name of God and perform all the Holy ordinances within the true Church of Jesus Christ. It is only bestowed upon worthy men through the laying on of hands by those commissioned by Jesus Christ. (5) The solid lines indicate divine authority and continued revelation with direct communication from Heaven. (6) The broken lines indicate connections, or off-shoots or developments of one movement or group of the Christian Churches to another as men made the changes without divine revelation, authority or sanction.

---

The grouping of the churches under the "Protestant Reformation" shows the great separatist movements at the top. The Church of England separated chiefly on political grounds. Lutheranism, Calvinism and Radical Sects Movements were born chiefly out of doctrinal and theological differences with the Roman Catholic Church.

From these four 16th Century movements many churches formed in Europe, came to America and separated from their parent bodies as indicated by the U. S. dates. The fans of broken lines shown in the chart represent independent churches in America which grew out of the reform movements, each line representing a single church. Those named, with the dates of their founding, are most of the large or historically important churches. Such a graph as this is an extreme simplification, attempting only to show each church in relation to the movement with which it is most closely connected.

On this "Square" (one square city block 630 ft. x 630 ft. or 10 acres) is located the Salt Lake Temple, which, as is the case in all Mormon Temples, is accessible only to Mormons in good standing. On this "Square" is also located the famous Tabernacle with its marvelous acoustics and organ.

From here also the world-renowned Tabernacle Choir broadcasts its music each Sunday morning, along with the "Spoken Sermonette." Brigham Young had a high wall erected around this Square, partly to furnish employment at the time and also to shield the area from traffic and other disturbances.

# World-Wide Headquarters of the Mormon Church

**CHURCH ADMINISTRATION BUILDING, Salt Lake City, Utah.**

Church Office Building, the administrative headquarters of the World-wide Mormon Church organization. The building contains the offices of the First Presidency (President and his two counselors).

It also houses offices of the members of the Quorum of the Twelve Apostles; the First Council of the Seventy; the Presiding Patriarch to the Church; the Presiding Bishopric; the Church Historian, and others.

Built of native Utah Granite, with interiors of marble and onyx, and beautiful and rare hard woods.

Representatives of Relief Societies of the nations at the time the new Relief Society building was dedicated at Salt Lake City, Utah, on October 3, 1956.

**RELIEF SOCIETY BUILDING, Salt Lake City, Utah.** From this beautiful structure, the Women's National Relief Society manages its world-wide organization.

Joseph Smith, Jr.
1830-1844

Brigham Young
1847-1877

# of Jesus Christ of Latter-day Saints
## a Prophet, Seer and Revelator

John Taylor
1880-1887

Wilford Woodruff
1889-1898

Lorenzo Snow
1898-1901

Joseph F. Smith
1901-1918

96

**Heber J. Grant
1918-1945**

**George Albert Smith
1945-1951**

**DAVID O. McKAY . . . 1951-**
Presidential, Prophet, Seer and Revelator of the Church of Jesus Christ of Latter-day Saints.

Henry D. Moyle
First Counselor

Hugh B. Brown
Second Counselor

# THE TWELVE APOSTLES OF THE MODERN-DAY CHURCH OF JESUS CHRIST

Joseph Fielding Smith

Harold B. Lee

Spencer W. Kimball

Ezra Taft Benson

Mark E. Petersen

Delbert L. Stapley

Marion G. Romney

LeGrand Richards

Richard L. Evans

Howard W. Hunter

Gordon B. Hinckley

N. Eldon Tanner

# The Church Functions

Priesthood members of the Church are here shown voting on important issues in the Tabernacle by raising their right hand. At each Annual and Semi-Annual Conference, both men and women vote in the same manner to sustain the Church Authorities.

# In a Democratic Way

All worthy male members 12 years of age and over are given some degree of Priesthood or divine authority to act in various capacities and functions in the Church. Likewise, all members, both male and female, of each local group or "Ward" vote periodically during the year to sustain or reject their leaders.

# ACTIVITY OF ALL MEMBERS . . . CONTRIBUTES TO DYNAMIC GROWTH AND SUCCESS OF THE CHURCH

Over one-half of the total adult membership of each "Ward" or local group hold responsible and active positions in its organizations.

The entire membership ot each "Ward" or group may participate in one or more of the following organizations, which meet regularly as shown below.

## ORGANIZATIONS and MEETINGS

**Priesthood Quorums** (Ordained male members; usually meet each Sunday morning)

| Division of Priesthood | Approx. Ages in Years | Number in Each Group |
|---|---|---|
| **Aaronic** | | |
| Deacons | 12-14 | 12 |
| Teachers | 15-17 | 24 |
| Priests | 17-19 | 48 |
| **Melchizedek** | | |
| Elders | 19 & over | 96 |
| Seventies | 21 & over | 70 |
| High Priests | 21 & over | Indefinite number |

### Sacrament Meeting
Attended by all ages, both male and female. Regular meeting held once each Sunday afternoon or evening.

### Sunday School
Attended by all ages, both male and female. Regular meeting held once each Sunday morning.

### Relief Society
Attended by women only. Ages from 18 years and over. Regular meetings weekly on a weekday.

### Mutual Improvement Associations
Attended by both male and female over 12 years of age. Regular meeting each week. (weekday evening)

### Primary Association
For children up to 12 years of age. Regular meeting weekday. (daytime)

## FUNCTIONS

These groups have the responsibility to direct all Church activities in their respective callings.

In their group activities they study all phases of religion; have group recreation, welfare and relief work.

Each Mormon family is visited briefly each month by "Ward Teachers" selected from these groups.

This is the main religious service for the entire membership of the Church. All partake of the Sacrament (bread and water) at this meeting.

Divided into age group classes. Members study all phases of religion. All partake of Sacrament (bread and water) at this meeting.

Study all phases of religion. In pairs they visit all members in their homes. Welfare work and care for needy and sick.

Study a variety of subjects. Special development of talents, drama, speech, etc. Recreation and dancing.

Study character and religious subjects. Recreation and play.

All leaders and teachers of the above organizations are volunteer non-paid workers (usually trained in some profession or trade at which they work during the day to sustain themselves).

**All of the above quorums, groups and organizations constitute the membership of a "Ward." Aaronic Priesthood quorums function entirely within a Ward. Melchizedek Priesthood quorums or groups meet and work within a Ward, but they also join like groups and quorums of other Wards to act as a "Stake" or larger group.**

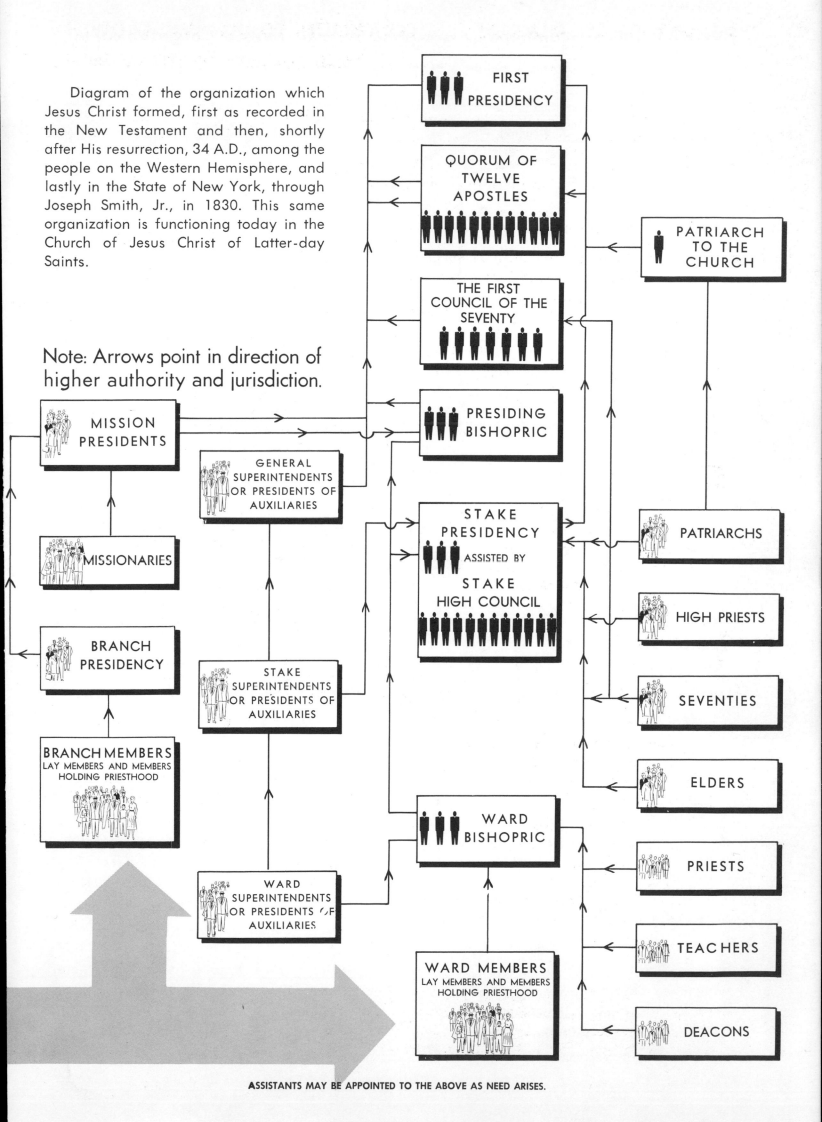

Diagram of the organization which Jesus Christ formed, first as recorded in the New Testament and then, shortly after His resurrection, 34 A.D., among the people on the Western Hemisphere, and lastly in the State of New York, through Joseph Smith, Jr., in 1830. This same organization is functioning today in the Church of Jesus Christ of Latter-day Saints.

Note: Arrows point in direction of higher authority and jurisdiction.

FIRST PRESIDENCY

QUORUM OF TWELVE APOSTLES

THE FIRST COUNCIL OF THE SEVENTY

PATRIARCH TO THE CHURCH

MISSION PRESIDENTS

GENERAL SUPERINTENDENTS OR PRESIDENTS OF AUXILIARIES

PRESIDING BISHOPRIC

STAKE PRESIDENCY ASSISTED BY STAKE HIGH COUNCIL

PATRIARCHS

MISSIONARIES

HIGH PRIESTS

BRANCH PRESIDENCY

STAKE SUPERINTENDENTS OR PRESIDENTS OF AUXILIARIES

SEVENTIES

BRANCH MEMBERS LAY MEMBERS AND MEMBERS HOLDING PRIESTHOOD

ELDERS

WARD BISHOPRIC

WARD SUPERINTENDENTS OR PRESIDENTS OF AUXILIARIES

PRIESTS

TEACHERS

WARD MEMBERS LAY MEMBERS AND MEMBERS HOLDING PRIESTHOOD

DEACONS

ASSISTANTS MAY BE APPOINTED TO THE ABOVE AS NEED ARISES.

# How the Church membership is organized and divided geographically.

## (Example below is in Los Angeles area, California)

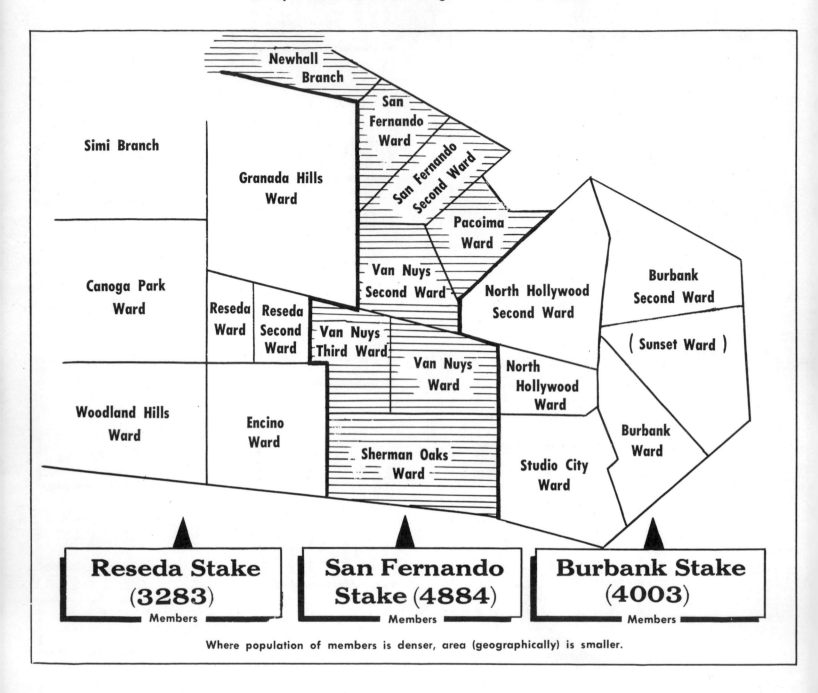

Simi Branch

Newhall Branch

San Fernando Ward

San Fernando Second Ward

Granada Hills Ward

Pacoima Ward

Canoga Park Ward

Reseda Ward

Reseda Second Ward

Van Nuys Second Ward

North Hollywood Second Ward

Burbank Second Ward

( Sunset Ward )

Van Nuys Third Ward

Van Nuys Ward

North Hollywood Ward

Woodland Hills Ward

Encino Ward

Sherman Oaks Ward

Studio City Ward

Burbank Ward

**Reseda Stake (3283)** Members

**San Fernando Stake (4884)** Members

**Burbank Stake (4003)** Members

Where population of members is denser, area (geographically) is smaller.

EACH "WARD" is comparable to a local congregation, parish, or single church.

Three or more wards make up a "Stake." The stake organization has supervisory functions over the activities of each ward.

Each ward group is made up geographically of from 200 to 900 persons. In areas with fewer Church members a smaller group may be called an "Independent Branch" or "Branch" and is under the jurisdiction of a stake or mission, respectively.

In any area where the Church members are not sufficient in numbers to organize into wards and stakes, the proselyting work, as well as the organizational functions of local groups, are carried on under the direction of a "Mission" organization, and its local unit or group is called a "Branch." Missions may have from three to one hundred or more branches, while a stake may have from three to fifteen wards (averaging about eight). Both "stake" and "mission" are arbitrary groupings.

104

**A typical Mormon church which is also called a ward.**

Each ward (or local unit) has an appropriate chapel, with organ and piano, for religious services of all Church organizations and groups. Also, each local unit or group has a recreation hall connecting onto or adjoining the chapel.

The recreation hall has many functions and uses. One or two nights a week it may be used as a gymnasium when various kinds of sports are played, such as basketball, volleyball and various gymnastics; or it may be appropriately decorated as a ballroom for social dancing; or again it may be turned into a theater and its stage used for dramatic presentations. Nearly all such recreation halls are also equipped so they may be used to show motion picture films, entertaining and educational.

Some activity, for various age groups, is usually going on four or five days and evenings weekly in nearly every ward chapel and recreation hall.

The Mormon program is to provide good recreation, under proper conditions and supervision, for all age groups, but especially for young people, so they will be less likely to seek it elsewhere under improper conditions.

There are many activities from which every member may choose, regardless of age. The social program of the Mormon Church is perhaps more extensive than that of any other church.

Representative recreation halls (auditoriums) which are used for sports, drama, and dancing, etc., are built next to or adjoining the chapel. Numerous classrooms are scattered throughout the buildings. There are in the Church more than 2,500 local units (chapels and recreation halls) such as these, and there are over 250 new ones being constructed in different parts of the world each year.

Mormon chapels and recreation halls are usually financed by the local group contributing one-half of the cost, either in donated labor or money or both, and the Church Headquarters contributing the other half. Tithing, or one-tenth of one's increase (in most cases income), is given voluntarily to the Church by its members. This is in addition to the contributions given to construct chapels and recreation halls.

**A young Mormon bishop (by profession a newspaper man) addressing his congregation.**

THE WARD or local group organization is presided over by a bishop and two counselors. All three spend only part time in directing their Church affairs. Although they direct and supervise all the Church activities in their ward, they also earn their living in whatever occupation they may be trained in, such as law, selling, plumbing, banking, etc.

The bishop and his counselors divide the work of conducting the various meetings and supervising the other organizations and activities of the ward. They in turn call others to help and give them responsibilities. In this way most of the membership of the ward ac-tively participate in either directing or working in one or more of the many organizations.

Every member of a ward over twelve years of age can have some assignment of work. The great majority of the members accept active responsibility. All work is voluntary, and none, including the choir members, conductor and organist, or even the bishop and his counselors, receive any monetary payment for their services.

A guest speaker or any member of the ward may be invited in any meeting to do the "preaching." Often non-Mormons are invited to give special talks. No one receives remuneration for such service.

**Music plays a big part in Mormon meetings.**

## WORSHIP • WORK • PLAY ALL PROVIDED FOR IN CHURCH BUILDING FACILITIES

Above is a "Fathers and Sons' " banquet. These, as well as "Mothers and Daughters' " activities are regular events throughout the Church.

## SPORTS • DRAMA • DANCING • BANQUETS

Each Ward (or local group) has a recreation hall adjoining the chapel. This recreation hall is used nearly every day and night in the week for some sport, stage play, musical, Boy Scout activity or banquet for any and all groups. The recreation hall thus serves as a gymnasium, theatre or banquet hall.

# M-MEN BASKETBALL PROGRAM . . .
## . . . LARGEST BASKETBALL LEAGUE IN THE WORLD

Nearly every ward produces a basketball team among its young men between the ages of 17 and 24. Playoffs among the teams of the wards of each stake bring the winning team to the divisional tournament. The annual all-Church finals is a tournament of the all-Church championship teams. Awards are given for the winning team on points, as well as for the team displaying the best sportsmanship.

Over 10,000 players participate in this program each year.

**The winners of an All-Church Tournament.**

**In Mormon philosophy the physical development of boys and girls and men and women is very important along with their spiritual, mental and moral development.**

# THE BIG QUESTION . . .

WITH SO MANY activities for all its members calling for leaders in so many fields — ministers to preach, leaders to organize, teachers to direct study, coaches for sports, scout leaders and full and part-time missionaries — where do the finances come from and how are they administered ?

The answer is simple. All serve voluntarily as part-time workers, receiving no money for their valuable services, with the exception of a relatively few General Church Leaders whose full-time services are needed. These few receive only a "living allowance."

Although members of the Church "tithe" themselves, nearly all the proceeds go to the building of chapels, recreation halls, temples, and the maintenance of these edifices. Also a tremendous welfare program is maintained for the providing of food, clothing, etc., for the dependent members. (See also page 136.)

The Mormons have found the solution — **All do some work — None do all the work.**

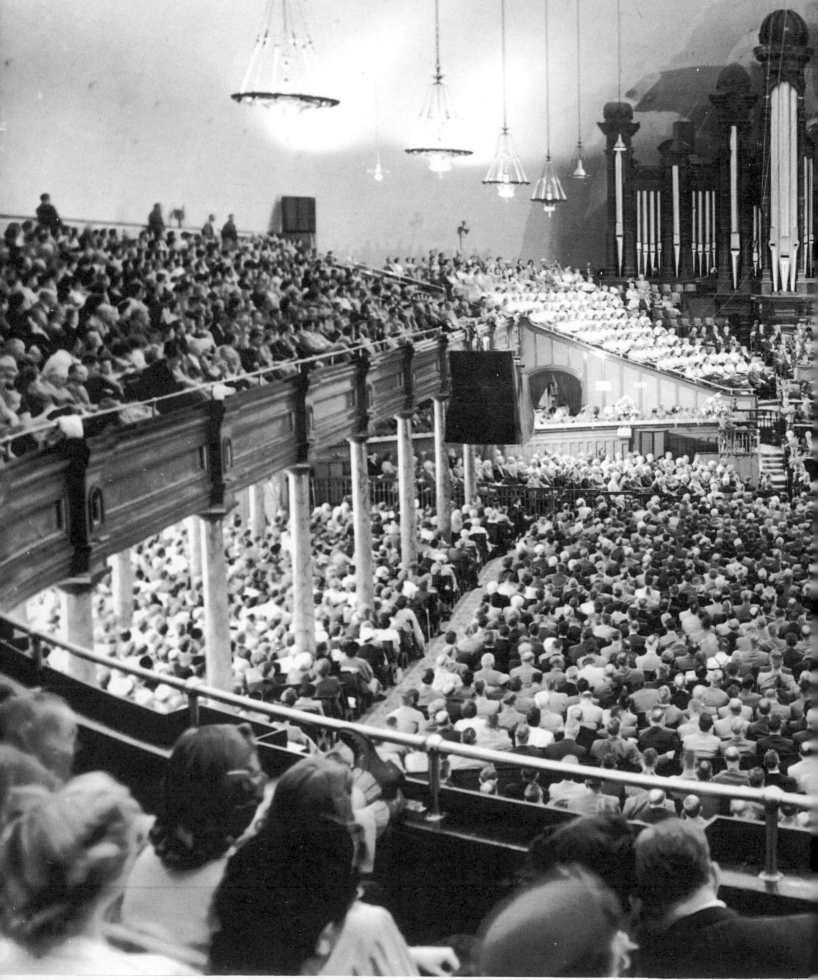

## GENERAL CONFERENCE

Twice each year the Church has a "General Conference." These annual and semi-annual assembly meetings are always held in Salt Lake City. These meetings continue for 112

three days, with sessions in the mornings and afternoons; special groups meet in the evenings. In the spring of the year Conference is held in April, with April 6th always included,

and in the fall of the year Conference is held in October.

The main services are held here in the Tabernacle on "Temple Square" with public address system connections in numerous other Church buildings located throughout several western states. Nearly all the meetings and proceedings are televised for the tens of thousands of people who are listening at home.

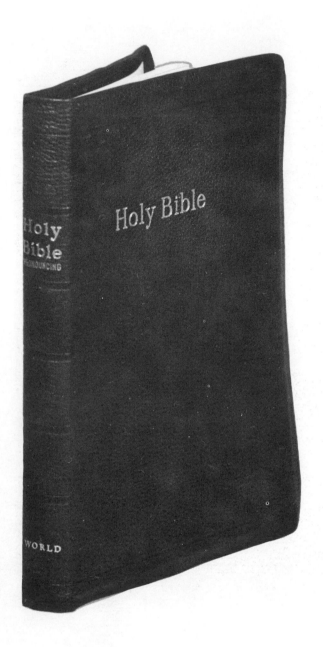

### The Bible

is the first of the "Four Standard Works" of the Mormon Church. In English, the King James version is the most widely used. Because of the manner in which the Bible has come down through the centuries, with errors in translations and interpretations of languages, the Church makes a reservation for its own interpretation as given in its "Articles of Faith," number 8: "We believe the Bible to be the word of God as far as it is translated correctly; . . ."

The Bible is a record of God's dealings with peoples on the Eastern Continent (Palestine, Egypt, etc.)

### The Book of Mormon

is the second of the four Standard Works of the Church. The Book of Mormon is a direct translation from ancient records (gold plates) of God's dealings with ancient peoples on the Western Continent (Americas). In number 8 of its Articles of Faith, the Church signifies the importance of this book: ": . . we also believe the Book of Mormon to be the word of God."

In the Book of Mormon, a record with detailed description is given of the appearance and visitation of Jesus Christ the Savior to the people on this the American Continent, following His death and resurrection in Jerusalem. This was His visit to His "other sheep" as spoken of in John 10:16.

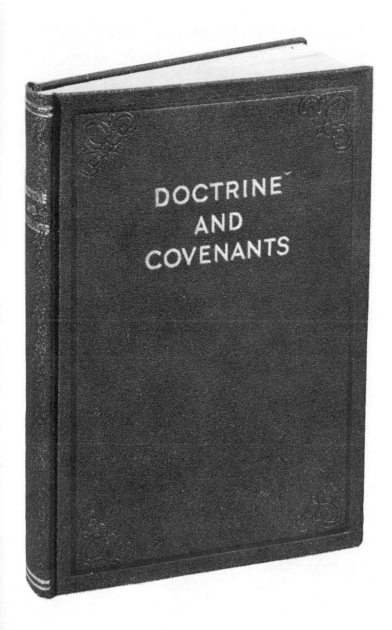

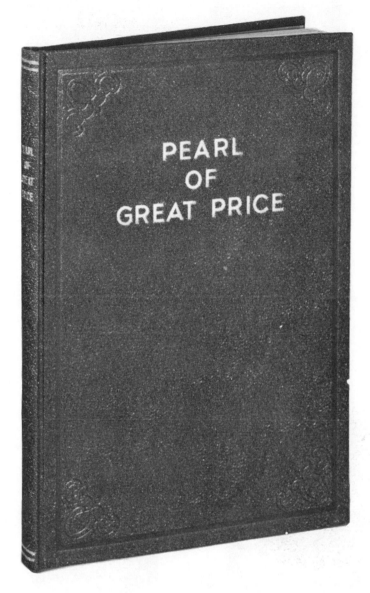

## The Doctrine and Covenants

or Book of Commandments contains modern-day revelations, written mostly verbatim as given by God to Joseph Smith. They deal with a great variety of subjects pertaining to the organization of the Church: its name; special instructions to many men in the beginning of its history; counsel on diet and health; explanations on the life to come; and instruction on the authority to act and perform ceremonies in the name of God, such as baptism, the laying on of hands for the gift of the Holy Ghost, and many others.

## The Pearl of Great Price

is the fourth of the "Four Standard Works" of the Church. It contains many selections from the revelations, translations, and narrations of Joseph Smith. The latter part or second section of the book contains a translation of some ancient records which came into Joseph Smith's possession. These records were on papyrus and came from the catacombs of Egypt. They are the words of Abraham, written by his own hand while he was in Egypt.

These papyri were later destroyed in the great Chicago fire.

This is a small volume, but contains such gems of knowledge as to make it truly a "Pearl of Great Price."

# Missionary Work . . .

## or sharing the wonders of the "Restored" Gospel of Christ with the world

IN MOST CHRISTIAN Churches, Missionary Work is carried on among non-Christian or "Heathen" peoples, to convert them to one form or another of Christianity. However, in the Mormon concept, missionary work is done among all peoples, both Christian and non-Christian, who are not Mormons.

They believe they have the complete Restored Gospel of Jesus Christ, which is so different from any other Christian or non-Christian church that missionary work, or the sharing of this complete Gospel of Christ with all peoples, is their accepted obligation and goal.

All capable and worthy adult members of the Mormon Church are possible candidates for missionary work and may be called as part-time or full-time missionary workers. A member doing missionary work supports himself (or herself) completely, through saving enough money beforehand, or his family or friends arrange to send part or all of the money to support him. A missionary's term averages two years wherever English is spoken, and two and a half years where a foreign language must be learned. Missionary work and missionaries are organized and supervised.

After the mission is completed, the member returns to his or her normal occupation or work, to pursue his or her daily livelihood, and others are called to carry on the missionary work.

There are from five to twelve thousand full-time (two or two and one-half years duration) missionaries, each self-supporting, who are in the "field" most of the time. There are also an approximately equal number of part-time missionaries, also entirely self-supporting, who work locally in areas around or close to their own homes.

**A group of missionaries about to depart for a 2 to 2½ year service to different places in the United States and many foreign countries.**

# STAKES & MISSIONS
### IN THE UNITED STATES
#### CHURCH OF JESUS CHRIST OF LATTER DAY SAINTS

EXPLANATION

MISSIONS – Any area where church membership is <u>less</u> concentrated

STAKES – Any area where church membership is <u>more</u> concentrated

Missionary work (proselyting) is carried on in both Missions and Stakes among all non-Mormons whether Catholic, Protestant or non-Christian.

NOTE
⊙ – Designates
      Mission Headquarters

(See descriptive definition and explanation of a "Stake" on page 104.)

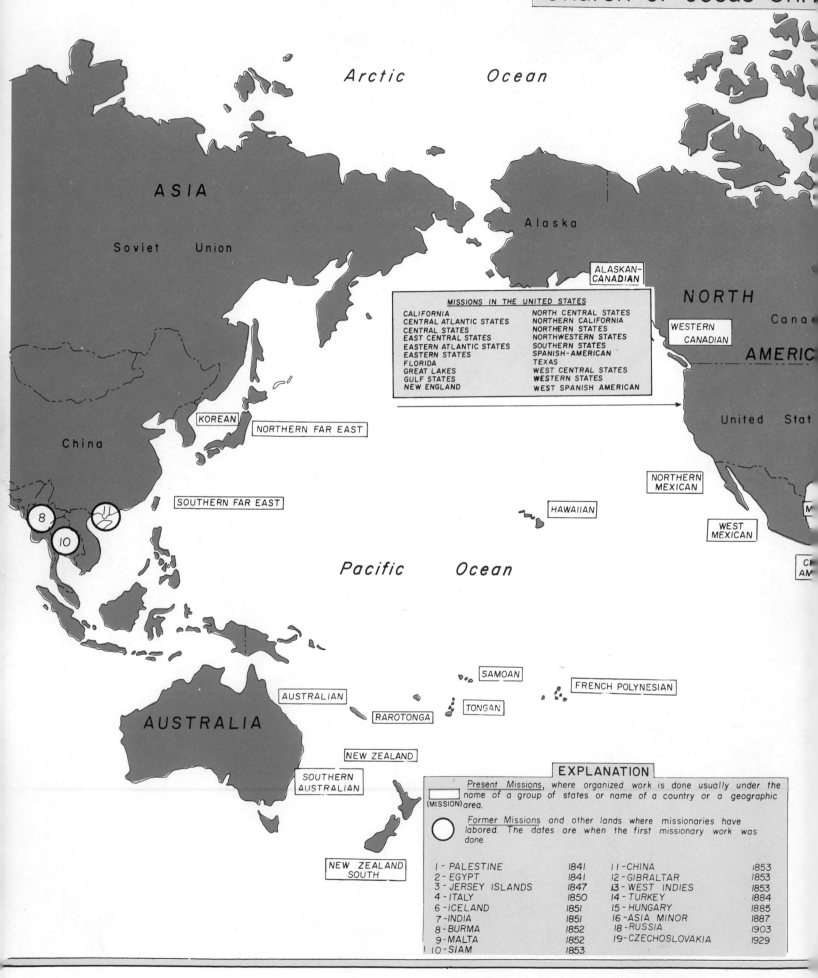

Arctic Ocean

ASIA

Soviet Union

Alaska

ALASKAN-CANADIAN

NORTH

WESTERN CANADIAN

AMERIC

Cana

**MISSIONS IN THE UNITED STATES**

| | |
|---|---|
| CALIFORNIA | NORTH CENTRAL STATES |
| CENTRAL ATLANTIC STATES | NORTHERN CALIFORNIA |
| CENTRAL STATES | NORTHERN STATES |
| EAST CENTRAL STATES | NORTHWESTERN STATES |
| EASTERN ATLANTIC STATES | SOUTHERN STATES |
| EASTERN STATES | SPANISH-AMERICAN |
| FLORIDA | TEXAS |
| GREAT LAKES | WEST CENTRAL STATES |
| GULF STATES | WESTERN STATES |
| NEW ENGLAND | WEST SPANISH AMERICAN |

KOREAN

NORTHERN FAR EAST

China

SOUTHERN FAR EAST

United Stat

⑧ 8

⑪ 11

⑩ 10

NORTHERN MEXICAN

HAWAIIAN

WEST MEXICAN

M

CI AM

Pacific Ocean

SAMOAN

FRENCH POLYNESIAN

AUSTRALIAN

TONGAN

RAROTONGA

AUSTRALIA

NEW ZEALAND

SOUTHERN AUSTRALIAN

## EXPLANATION

Present Missions, where organized work is done usually under the name of a group of states or name of a country or a geographic area.
(MISSION)

○ Former Missions and other lands where missionaries have labored. The dates are when the first missionary work was done.

NEW ZEALAND SOUTH

| | | | | | |
|---|---|---|---|---|---|
| 1 - PALESTINE | 1841 | | 11 - CHINA | 1853 |
| 2 - EGYPT | 1841 | | 12 - GIBRALTAR | 1853 |
| 3 - JERSEY ISLANDS | 1847 | | 13 - WEST INDIES | 1853 |
| 4 - ITALY | 1850 | | 14 - TURKEY | 1884 |
| 6 - ICELAND | 1851 | | 15 - HUNGARY | 1885 |
| 7 - INDIA | 1851 | | 16 - ASIA MINOR | 1887 |
| 8 - BURMA | 1852 | | 18 - RUSSIA | 1903 |
| 9 - MALTA | 1852 | | 19 - CZECHOSLOVAKIA | 1929 |
| 10 - SIAM | 1853 | | | |

# MISSIONS

of Latter Day Saints

GREENLAND

EUROPE

(6)

NORTHEAST BRITISH
SCOTTISH
NORTH BRITISH
IRISH
CENTRAL BRITISH
SOUTHWEST BRITISH
BRITISH
FRENCH

FRENCH
EAST

NORWEGIAN

SWEDISH

DANISH

FINNISH

(18)

NETHERLANDS
NORTH GERMAN
CENTRAL GERMAN
WEST GERMAN
SWISS
AUSTRIAN

BERLIN

SOUTH GERMAN

(19)

(15)

BAVARIAN

(3)

(4)

(14) (16)

(9)

(1)

(12)

(2)

(7)
India

CANADIAN

Atlantic          Ocean

(3)

AFRICA

Indian

Ocean

SOUTH

BRAZILIAN

AMERICA

ANDES

CHILEAN

BRAZILIAN SOUTH

ARGENTINE
NORTH

URUGUAY

ARGENTINE

SOUTH
AFRICAN

# The Famous Mormon Tabernacle Choir . . .

**375 TESTED VOICES . . . HOUSEWIVES — DOCTORS — LAWYE**

TEACHERS — LABORERS — BUSINESSMEN — TRADESMEN

# SOME OF THE "FRUITS" OF MORMONISM IN THE FIELD OF EDUCATION AND TRAINING

## EDUCATIONAL STATUS OF THE POPULATION
### Median School Years Completed by Persons 25 Years of Age and Older

According to the U. S. Bureau of the Census, persons 25 years old and older had, on the average, a little more than nine years of formal schooling—9.3 years.

Only one state—Utah—can boast that on the average its people 25 years old and older had a high-school education or its equivalent.

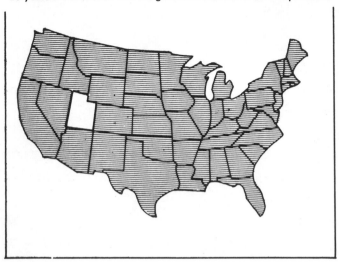

## UTAH HAS THE HIGHEST PERCENTAGE IN THE NATION OF ITS TOTAL POPULATION IN SCHOOL

Utah's elementary and secondary education load, as measured by the percentage of the total population enrolled in public schools is highest in the entire nation.

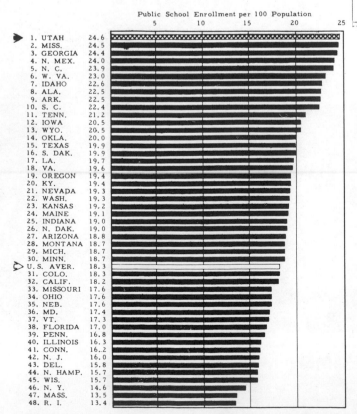

Public School Enrollment per 100 Population

| |  |  |
|---|---|---|
| 1. | UTAH | 24.6 |
| 2. | MISS. | 24.5 |
| 3. | GEORGIA | 24.4 |
| 4. | N. MEX. | 24.0 |
| 5. | N. C. | 23.9 |
| 6. | W. VA. | 23.0 |
| 7. | IDAHO | 22.6 |
| 8. | ALA. | 22.5 |
| 9. | ARK. | 22.5 |
| 10. | S. C. | 22.4 |
| 11. | TENN. | 21.2 |
| 12. | IOWA | 20.5 |
| 13. | WYO. | 20.5 |
| 14. | OKLA. | 20.0 |
| 15. | TEXAS | 19.9 |
| 16. | S. DAK. | 19.9 |
| 17. | LA. | 19.7 |
| 18. | VA. | 19.6 |
| 19. | OREGON | 19.4 |
| 20. | KY. | 19.4 |
| 21. | NEVADA | 19.3 |
| 22. | WASH. | 19.3 |
| 23. | KANSAS | 19.2 |
| 24. | MAINE | 19.1 |
| 25. | INDIANA | 19.0 |
| 26. | N. DAK. | 19.0 |
| 27. | ARIZONA | 18.8 |
| 28. | MONTANA | 18.7 |
| 29. | MICH. | 18.7 |
| 30. | MINN. | 18.7 |
| | U. S. AVER. | 18.3 |
| 31. | COLO. | 18.3 |
| 32. | CALIF. | 18.2 |
| 33. | MISSOURI | 17.6 |
| 34. | OHIO | 17.6 |
| 35. | NEB. | 17.6 |
| 36. | MD. | 17.4 |
| 37. | VT. | 17.3 |
| 38. | FLORIDA | 17.0 |
| 39. | PENN. | 16.8 |
| 40. | ILLINOIS | 16.3 |
| 41. | CONN. | 16.2 |
| 42. | N. J. | 16.0 |
| 43. | DEL. | 15.8 |
| 44. | N. HAMP. | 15.7 |
| 45. | WIS. | 15.7 |
| 46. | N. Y. | 14.6 |
| 47. | MASS. | 13.5 |
| 48. | R. I. | 13.4 |

## UTAH TOPS NATION IN EFFORT

Utah leads the entire nation in effort to support public schools. The state's people spend a larger proportion of their personal income for public schools than do the people of any other state. According to the latest official U. S. Office of Education data, Utahns spent $4.09 out of every $100 in individual income for state and local school taxes. This compares with a national average of $2.56 and an average of $3.30 in the eight Mountain States. The fact that Utah has such a high proportion of its total population in the public schools is a major factor accounting for Utah's heavy tax load.

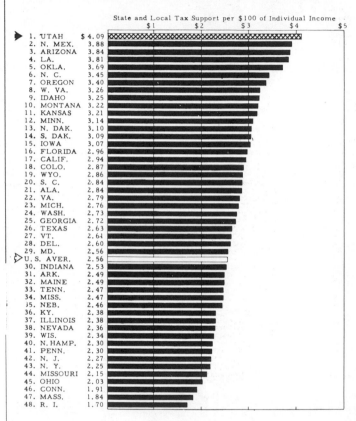

State and Local Tax Support per $100 of Individual Income

| |  |  |
|---|---|---|
| 1. | UTAH | $4.09 |
| 2. | N. MEX. | 3.88 |
| 3. | ARIZONA | 3.84 |
| 4. | LA. | 3.81 |
| 5. | OKLA. | 3.69 |
| 6. | N. C. | 3.45 |
| 7. | OREGON | 3.40 |
| 8. | W. VA. | 3.26 |
| 9. | IDAHO | 3.25 |
| 10. | MONTANA | 3.22 |
| 11. | KANSAS | 3.21 |
| 12. | MINN. | 3.14 |
| 13. | N. DAK. | 3.10 |
| 14. | S. DAK. | 3.09 |
| 15. | IOWA | 3.07 |
| 16. | FLORIDA | 2.96 |
| 17. | CALIF. | 2.94 |
| 18. | COLO. | 2.87 |
| 19. | WYO. | 2.86 |
| 20. | S. C. | 2.84 |
| 21. | ALA. | 2.84 |
| 22. | VA. | 2.79 |
| 23. | MICH. | 2.76 |
| 24. | WASH. | 2.73 |
| 25. | GEORGIA | 2.72 |
| 26. | TEXAS | 2.63 |
| 27. | VT. | 2.61 |
| 28. | DEL. | 2.60 |
| 29. | MD. | 2.56 |
| | U. S. AVER. | 2.56 |
| 30. | INDIANA | 2.53 |
| 31. | ARK. | 2.49 |
| 32. | MAINE | 2.49 |
| 33. | TENN. | 2.47 |
| 34. | MISS. | 2.47 |
| 35. | NEB. | 2.46 |
| 36. | KY. | 2.38 |
| 37. | ILLINOIS | 2.38 |
| 38. | NEVADA | 2.36 |
| 39. | WIS. | 2.34 |
| 40. | N. HAMP. | 2.30 |
| 41. | PENN. | 2.30 |
| 42. | N. J. | 2.27 |
| 43. | N. Y. | 2.25 |
| 44. | MISSOURI | 2.15 |
| 45. | OHIO | 2.03 |
| 46. | CONN. | 1.91 |
| 47. | MASS. | 1.84 |
| 48. | R. I. | 1.70 |

## SELECTIVE SERVICE REGISTRANTS FAILING THE AFQ TEST

Utah had the lowest percentage in the nation of Selective Service registrants who failed the Armed Forces Qualification Test during the Korean War.

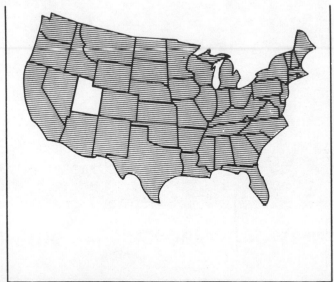

SOURCE: Prepared by Utah Foundation from official reports of the U. S. Office of Education and the U. S. Department of Commerce.

# MORMON EDUCATIONAL STANDARDS HIGH

ONE OF THE main principles of Mormon belief is that a person cannot be saved in ignorance, or that a person is saved no faster than he gains righteous knowledge. In other words, education, or the acquiring of knowledge in all fields, is a necessary prerequisite to the exhaltation of the soul. This is one of the principles in which the Mormons differ from most other denominations.

Mormons do not believe that it is by the grace of God alone that men are saved. Their belief in this matter of salvation of the soul agrees with the Apostle Paul's declarations, that the "works" of the individual are as necessary as his faith; and that both faith and works — which they interpret as righteous living and the acquiring of knowledge — are necessary for man's happiness in this life and his salvation in the life to come.

The Mormons believe that salvation is a matter of degree to the extent that knowledge, righteously applied in living, will increase one's capacity to "inherit" or earn a greater degree of salvation or exaltation.

This belief and thinking gives rise to a very ambitious program of education throughout the whole of a Mormon's life. Thus a person who is diligent in gaining knowledge and developing himself intellectually, morally and spiritually, has an advantage over one who is not so diligent. All of this spurs educational activity and endeavor to a very high degree among the Mormons.

The state of Utah, because of its concentration of Mormon population, may be used to show the results of such a philosophy in action among the Mormons. The figures here shown might be even more contrasting if the whole population of Utah were Mormon. Salt Lake City, Utah's largest city and most thickly populated area, is about 45% non-Mormon. Nevertheless, it is interesting to see how the theory of education of the Mormon Church has affected the educational standards of the whole state.

## PERCENT OF PERSONS OF VOTING AGE VOTING IN PRESIDENTIAL ELECTION

Educators agree that one objective of education is good citizenship. This objective has many different meanings, one of them being voting intelligently on candidates for public office. While local or statewide elections often are of more concern to the voters, a Presidential election being nationwide shows the comparative interest of the voters of the various states. In the nation as a whole 65.3 percent of the prospective voters voted; among the states the range was from 79.6 percent in Utah to 24.3 percent in Mississippi.

Research has shown that generally the more formal schooling a person has the more likely it is that he will cast his vote. Utah had the largest percent of voters voting. It has the highest educational attainment among adults—12.0 years of schooling.

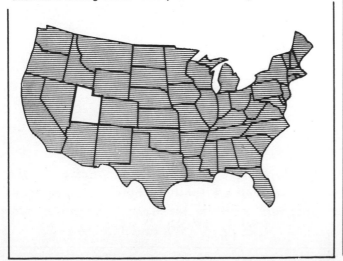

## PERCENT OF TOTAL SCHOOL ENROLLMENT IN NONPUBLIC SCHOOLS (DENOMINATIONAL AND NONSECTARIAN) IN THE 48 STATES

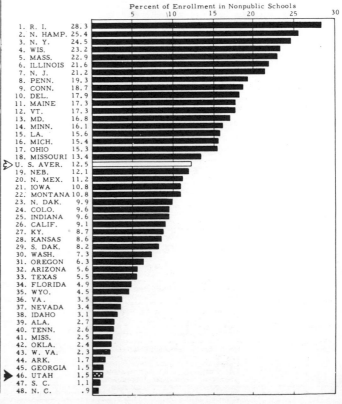

Percent of Enrollment in Nonpublic Schools

| | | |
|---|---|---|
| 1. R. I. | 28.3 | |
| 2. N. HAMP. | 25.4 | |
| 3. N. Y. | 24.5 | |
| 4. WIS. | 23.2 | |
| 5. MASS. | 22.9 | |
| 6. ILLINOIS | 21.6 | |
| 7. N. J. | 21.2 | |
| 8. PENN. | 19.3 | |
| 9. CONN. | 18.7 | |
| 10. DEL. | 17.9 | |
| 11. MAINE | 17.3 | |
| 12. VT. | 17.3 | |
| 13. MD. | 16.8 | |
| 14. MINN. | 16.1 | |
| 15. LA. | 15.6 | |
| 16. MICH. | 15.4 | |
| 17. OHIO | 15.3 | |
| 18. MISSOURI | 13.4 | |
| U. S. AVER. | 12.5 | |
| 19. NEB. | 12.1 | |
| 20. N. MEX. | 11.2 | |
| 21. IOWA | 10.8 | |
| 22. MONTANA | 10.8 | |
| 23. N. DAK. | 9.9 | |
| 24. COLO. | 9.6 | |
| 25. INDIANA | 9.6 | |
| 26. CALIF. | 9.1 | |
| 27. KY. | 8.7 | |
| 28. KANSAS | 8.6 | |
| 29. S. DAK. | 8.2 | |
| 30. WASH. | 7.3 | |
| 31. OREGON | 6.3 | |
| 32. ARIZONA | 5.6 | |
| 33. TEXAS | 5.5 | |
| 34. FLORIDA | 4.9 | |
| 35. WYO. | 4.5 | |
| 36. VA. | 3.5 | |
| 37. NEVADA | 3.4 | |
| 38. IDAHO | 3.1 | |
| 39. ALA. | 2.7 | |
| 40. TENN. | 2.6 | |
| 41. MISS. | 2.5 | |
| 42. OKLA. | 2.4 | |
| 43. W. VA. | 2.3 | |
| 44. ARK. | 1.7 | |
| 45. GEORGIA | 1.5 | |
| 46. UTAH | 1.5 | |
| 47. S. C. | 1.1 | |
| 48. N. C. | .9 | |

# A FORMAL STATEMENT ON "MORMON" DOCTRINE

IN THE MONTH of March, 1841, Mr. John Wentworth, editor of the Chicago Democrat, wrote to Joseph Smith asking him to explain the "Mormon" Church and its principles.

Joseph Smith's answer to Mr. Wentworth was in the form of a letter of nearly six pages, in which he related the main events in connection with the history, organization and development of the Church, beginning with his birth and ending March, 1841, a period of thirty-six years.

Near the end of Joseph Smith's letter to Mr. Wentworth, he sets out in clear and simple terms the Mormon's religious creed, in what has since become known as the "Articles of Faith" of the Church of Jesus Christ of Latter-day Saints.

The principles of the Church as set out in the thirteen Articles of Faith cover the main points of doctrine of the Church.

Doctrines of the Church are to be found in detail in the books illustrated on pp. 114, 115.

# The Articles of Faith
## Of the Church of Jesus Christ of Latter-day Saints

**1. We believe in God, the Eternal Father, and in His Son, Jesus Christ, and in the Holy Ghost.**
(See pp. 12-14 and 138.)

**4. We believe that the first principles and ordinances of the Gospel are:** first, **Faith in the Lord Jesus Christ;** second, **Repentence;** third, **Baptism by immersion for the remission of sins;** fourth, **Laying on of hands for the gift of the Holy Ghost.**
(See p. 27.)

**2. We believe that men will be punished for their own sins, and not for Adam's transgression.** (See doctrines found in books on pp. 114, 115.)

**5. We believe that a man must be called of God, by prophecy, and by the laying on of hands, by those who are in authority to preach the Gospel and administer in the ordinances thereof.** (See pp. 26-28.)

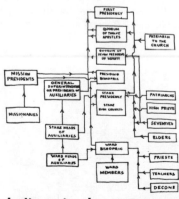

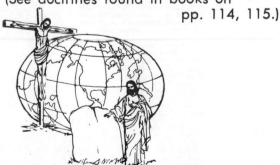

**3. We believe that through the Atonement of Christ, all mankind may be saved by obedience to the laws and ordinances of the Gospel.**
124 (See p. 80.)

**6. We believe in the same organization that existed in the Primitive Church, viz., apostles, prophets, pastors, teachers, evangelists, etc.**
(See pp. 29, 89, and 102-103.)

**7.** We believe in the gift of tongues, prophecy, revelation, visions, healing, interpretation of tongues, etc. (See pp. 8-9, 13, 16, 27.)

**11.** We claim the privilege of worshiping Almighty God according to the dictates of our own conscience, and allow all men the same privilege, let them worship how, where, or what they may.     (See pp. 160- 161.)

**8.** We believe the Bible to be the word of God as far as it is translated correctly; we also believe the Book of Mormon to be the word of God.     (See pp. 17-25 and 114-115.)

**12.** We believe in being subject to kings, presidents, rulers, and magistrates, in obeying, honoring, and sustaining the law.
(See pp. 140, 146, 158.)

**9.** We believe all that God has revealed, all that He does now reveal, and we believe that He will yet reveal many great and important things pertaining to the Kingdom of God.
(See pp. 114-115.)

**10.** We believe in the literal gathering of Israel and in the restoration of the Ten Tribes; that Zion will be built upon this (the American) continent; that Christ will reign personally upon the earth; and that the earth will be renewed and receive its paradisiacal glory.
(See pp. 66, 67, 88.)

**13.** We believe in being honest, true, chaste, benevolent, virtuous, and in doing good to all men; indeed, we may say that we follow the admonition of Paul—We believe all things, we hope all things, we have endured many things, and hope to be able to endure all things. If there is anything virtuous, lovely, or of good report or praiseworthy, we seek after these things.—

**JOSEPH SMITH**

# TYPICAL HIGH SCHOOLS IN UTAH . . .

⇧ **Ogden High School**
**Ogden, Utah**

**Olympus High School**
**Salt Lake City, Utah** ⇩

 Jordan High School
Near Salt Lake City, Utah

Cyprus High School
Magna, Utah

## The University of Utah
### Salt Lake City, Utah

Was formerly established under the name of "University of Deseret." The second law enacted by the Legislative Assembly of the State of "Deseret" was that of creating a university. The law was passed February 28, 1850, less than three years after the first Pioneers entered the Salt Lake Valley. This was one of the first universities west of the Mississippi River. The Mormons have considered education of primary importance from the very beginning. Joseph Smith declared that "the Glory of God is intelligence," "Seek knowledge out of the best books of the land," and that "Man cannot be saved in ignorance." To-day the University of Utah has an enrollment on the college level of over 10,000 students. Above is an air view of its rapidly expanding campus. It is strictly a state institution and is not under any jurisdiction of the Church.

 **Brigham Young University**
Provo, Utah

Was founded by the Church in 1875 under the name of Brigham Young Academy, which title was subsequently changed to the Brigham Young University. Today it has a student enrollment of nearly 15,000 on the college level. One need not be a member of the "Mormon" Church to attend. This University is owned and controlled by the Church.

**Utah State University**
Logan, Utah

Was founded in 1890. It is outstanding in agricultural subjects. It has received national recognition in the field of forestry. The total student enrollment on the college level is over 5,000.

# RELIGIOUS SEMINARIES

ALTHOUGH the Mormons have fewer students in parochial or private schools in Utah than any other state in the United States, except North and South Carolina, they afford opportunity for their young people on the high school and college level to study religion. Buildings appropriately built and conveniently located provide Seminaries and Institutes of Religion.

These are located just off the campus of nearly every high school, college and university in Utah and other states where enough Mormon students are enrolled in public institutions to warrant their construction. The religious instruction in Seminaries is usually given before and after the regular school classroom periods. The New and Old Testament of the Bible are studied, as well as Church History, the Book of Mormon, and related subjects. Enrollment is entirely voluntary.

As every Mormon boy or girl may receive a call to fulfill a mission, such training, along with their Church activities, helps to better equip them in teaching and sharing with others the Mormon philosophy of life.

**L. D. S. Institute, University of Utah, Salt Lake City, Utah.**

**L. D. S. Ogden Seminary**
**Ogden, Utah**

**L. D. S. Logan Institute**
**Logan, Utah**

**L. D. S. Seminary**
**Mesa, Arizona**

**L. D. S. Seminary**
**Payson, Utah**

**L. D. S. Kaysville Seminary**
**Kaysville, Utah**

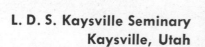

# The Mormons Are a Home-Loving People

UTAH IS ONE of the highest states in the nation in percentage of home owners. Nearly 75% of the people of Utah own or are buying their own homes.

On these two pages are shown some various types of homes that may be seen throughout Utah and in Mormon communities in other states.

# Mormons Are Healthy

## Here are some of the reasons . . .

### Their Moral Code . . .

"Our body is the tabernacle of a spiritual child of God. It must be kept as pure as possible. The body of man constitutes the earthly 'housing' for the eternal personal spirit of man and this eternal spirit can express itself only through that body; therefore a healthy body is of primary importance. Conversely, to defile man's body, in any degree, is to hamper the free operation of man's own personal eternal spirit."

They severely believe in a single standard of marriage — husband and wife each held accountable equally to be faithful in all matters concerning morals. Adultery, by either spouse, is grounds for being disfellowshipped from the Church.

A healthy mind and a healthy body are among the prime objectives in Mormon teaching.

### Their Health Code . . .

Over a hundred years ago the Prophet Joseph Smith, seeking to know what foods and drink were good for the body, received a revelation from God (February 27, 1833, at Kirtland, Ohio). This is known as the "Word of Wisdom." In part it says — or implies:

Eat wisely and understandingly.

Take into your body only the things that will build it.

Eat meat sparingly and then preferably during the cold time of the year.

Eat vegetables freely.

Eat fruits freely.

All grains are good, but specific grains are better for animals, such as oats for the horse, corn for the ox, rye for the fowls and swine; but WHEAT is best for man.

**Moderation** is perhaps the keynote in this code of living. Foods we **need** should become the foods we desire.

### Some of the don'ts:

Abstain from taking tobacco into the body in any form. Tobacco is to be used as a medicine for sick cattle, and its by-product, nicotine, is to be used for sick cattle and as an insecticide.

Abstain from any drink containing alcohol. Alcohol is for the washing and the use of the body **outside,** not inside.

Avoid **hot drinks.** This is generally understood to mean any drink that is habit forming or contains unnatural stimulating substances.

### Such a high and strict code of morals and health should produce results. . . .

Utah's birth rate is the highest and its death rate the lowest among the various states, and in between these two, the Mormons enjoy a greater degree of vitality, vigor and health than any other single group of people of comparable size.

# The Church Welfare Plan and Program

THE WELFARE PLAN of the Mormon Church is a combination Red Cross, Flood and Disaster Relief, Employment Service and Community Chest. It affords immediate "cure" in times of disaster and has a long-range program for individual preparedness which may act as a "preventive" to meet emergencies as they may arise. It is based on the Christian concept that **"we are our brother's keeper."**

Every true Latter-day Saint (Mormon) believes that God requires the membership of His Church to look after the temporal wants of its needy members so that none shall suffer for the necessities of life.

For the purpose of administering the Welfare Program, stakes in natural geographical areas are organized into regions.

The stake organization coordinates the work of the wards in the stake. The regional organization coordinates the work of the stakes in a region, and a General Church Welfare Committee, under the direction of the First Presidency of the Church, coordinates the welfare work throughout the Church.

Upon the bishop of each ward the Lord placed the responsibility to look after the poor. He, with the help of his counselors and the ward Relief Society Presidency, directs the work in the ward.

Almost from its beginning, the Church has observed a monthly Fast Day. The Church teaches its members to abstain from eating two meals on this day — the first Sunday of the month — and to contribute voluntarily in cash to the bishop the equivalent of these two meals. For the observance of this practice, the Lord has promised great spiritual and temporal blessings. Properly observed, the practice

puts in the hands of bishops a sizeable sum with which to meet the cash requirements of the needy.

Projects are now in operation producing such basic necessities of life as grains and grain products, meats, dairy and poultry products, fruits, vegetables, clothing, fuel, furniture, bedding, and the like. These projects are fostered through voluntary contributions of Church members and their friends. They provide opportunities where those needing help can labor for what they receive, thus removing from them the injurious effects of a dole.

The products produced by the welfare organizations are not for sale. They are cared for in storehouses known as Bishops' Storehouses, established exclusively for that purpose. All goods, foods and materials are distributed on Bishops' Orders to the worthy poor on the basis of need.

A great many Church members who do not need help, donate time each week and go to Church-owned farms and factories to raise and process foods, clothing and other necessities of life, from which they themselves receive no direct temporal benefit. This may be done either during daytime or night, as the program requires. Busy members are asked and encouraged to take time off from their usual daily occupations to help in the welfare program.

Men, women and children all participate, contributing their time and money to share in this program.

To be prepared for a "rainy day" or whatever may come to disrupt orderly and normal living, the Church leaders have also advised each family to store sufficient nutritious foods to last for one or two years as circumstances of the individual members permit.

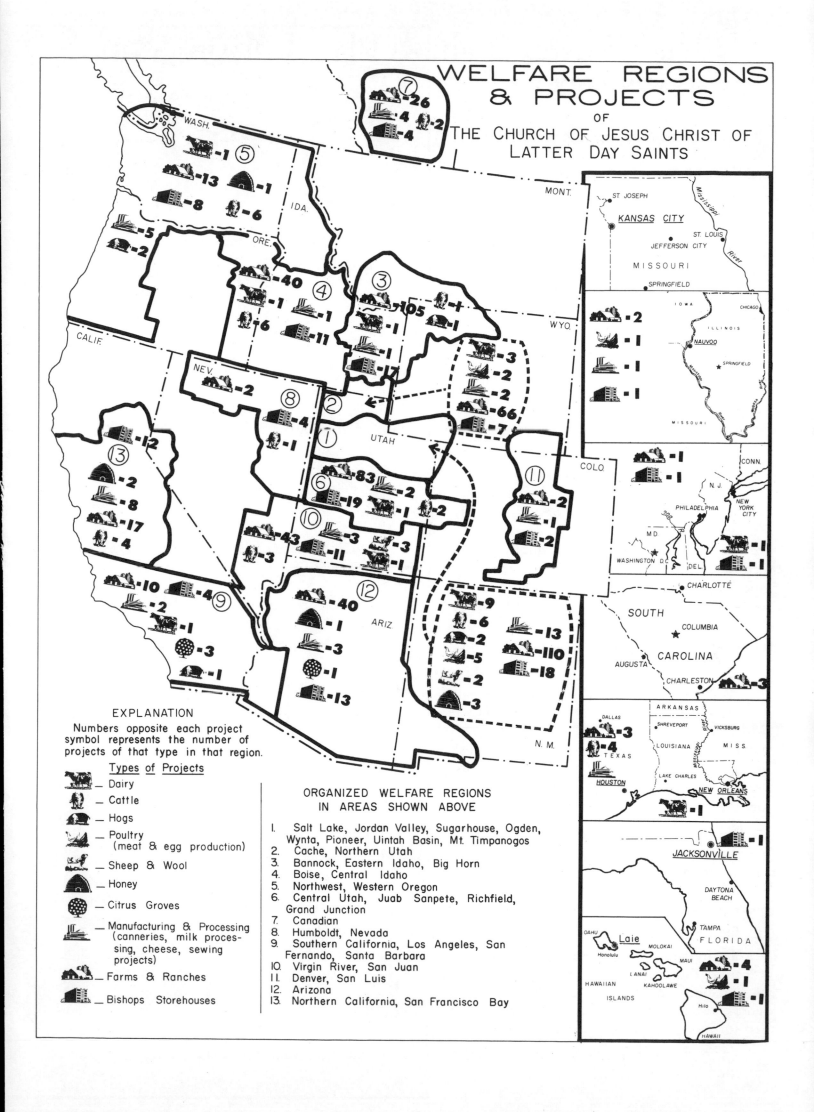

# WELFARE REGIONS & PROJECTS
## OF
## THE CHURCH OF JESUS CHRIST OF LATTER DAY SAINTS

## EXPLANATION

Numbers opposite each project symbol represents the number of projects of that type in that region.

### Types of Projects

- Dairy
- Cattle
- Hogs
- Poultry (meat & egg production)
- Sheep & Wool
- Honey
- Citrus Groves
- Manufacturing & Processing (canneries, milk processing, cheese, sewing projects)
- Farms & Ranches
- Bishops Storehouses

## ORGANIZED WELFARE REGIONS IN AREAS SHOWN ABOVE

1. Salt Lake, Jordan Valley, Sugarhouse, Ogden, Wynta, Pioneer, Uintah Basin, Mt. Timpanogos
2. Cache, Northern Utah
3. Bannock, Eastern Idaho, Big Horn
4. Boise, Central Idaho
5. Northwest, Western Oregon
6. Central Utah, Juab Sanpete, Richfield, Grand Junction
7. Canadian
8. Humboldt, Nevada
9. Southern California, Los Angeles, San Fernando, Santa Barbara
10. Virgin River, San Juan
11. Denver, San Luis
12. Arizona
13. Northern California, San Francisco Bay

## MORMON THEOLOGY

THE MORMON Church's concept of God, and man's relationship to Him, is different from that of any other Christian or non-Christian Church.

In the beginning of the recorded history of man, as found in the Old Testament — in which the Mormons firmly believe — God the Creator appeared and conversed frequently with His chosen prophets on the earth. This they believe in a literal sense. Through the centuries righteousness among the inhabitants of the earth has come and gone in irregular periods. When man in humility, and with sufficient faith, called upon God, and a divine purpose could be fulfilled, God revealed Himself and many times actually appeared and spoke to him.

The Mormons believe the personality of God is that of an actual embodied personal Being in whose very image man was literally created. Although most churches and religious groups as such, officially or formally define God as a "Spirit incorporeal and without definite form or substance," countless numbers of people, of all faiths, "visualize" God to be, as do the Mormons, a perfect embodied personage and not just a spirit or spiritual substance without form or shape.

The Holy Trinity, to the Mormons, consists of three distinct and separate personages — God the Father, Jesus Christ the Son, both possessing perfect bodies of immortal flesh and bone, and the Holy Ghost, the third member, a personage of spirit but separate in identity from the Father and the Son.

Mormon Theology is based upon this understanding as given to Joseph Smith when in the spring of 1820, near Palmyra, New York, God the Father and Jesus Christ appeared and conversed with him (see Joseph Smith's story in forepart of this book).

The tremendous importance the Mormons attach to this clarification and understanding of God and the Godhead is expressed in the words of Jesus (John 17:3): "And this is life eternal, that they might know Thee the only true God, and Jesus Christ whom Thou hast sent."

138

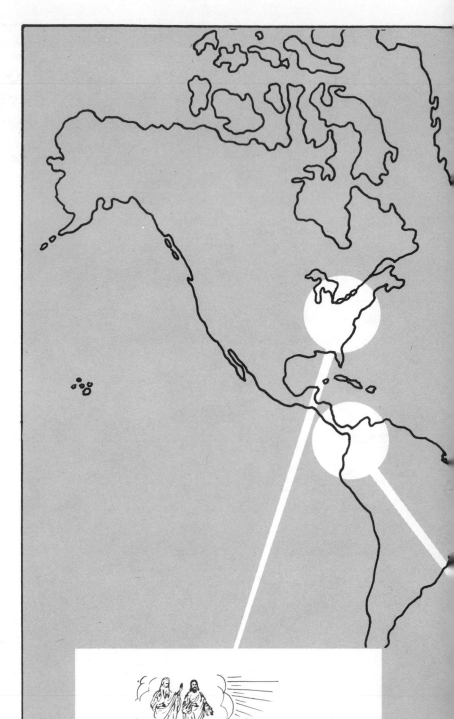

God the Father and Jesus Christ the Son together appeared to Joseph Smith, Jr., in the Spring of 1820 near Palmyra, New York State. This astounding event is described in detail in "Joseph Smith's Own Story."

# THE RECORDED APPEARANCES OF GOD THE FATHER AND JESUS CHRIST, HIS SON, TO PERSONS UPON THE EARTH

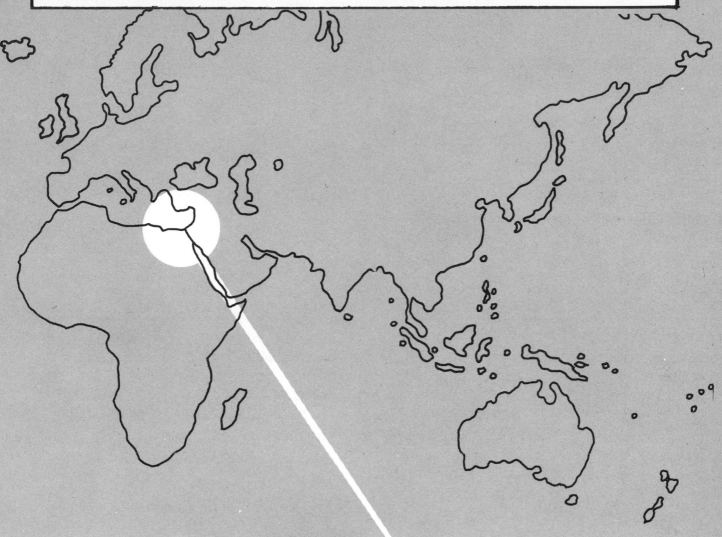

**J**esus Christ shortly after His resurrection fulfilled His own declaration and prophesy, as recorded in John 10:16 in the New Testament, when He said, "Other sheep I have which are not of this fold, them also I must bring and they shall hear my voice." . . . This visit of Jesus Christ among the people of the Americas is recorded in the 3rd Book of Nephi in the Book of Mormon.

**O**ld Testament recordings of God "Jehovah" appearing to Moses, Abraham and others.

Also Jesus, the only begotten Son of God the Father, lived, died and lived again after His resurrection in this area. Both God the Father and Jesus Christ, His Son, as two distinct personages, were seen by Stephen at the time of his being stoned, as recorded in the New Testament.

# Oh Yes,

## Polygamy Is Part of the Mormon Story

THE ANNOUNCEMENT and subsequent practice of the doctrine of polygamy by Joseph Smith to his followers, was a very serious and grave undertaking. Some sensational journalism and lurid writings have given the world an inaccurate and misleading story of Mormon polygamy.

Many wierd tales on polygamy among the Mormons were "fed" to the public in earlier times, and even now and then an article or novel may appear in the press that rehashes the old tales of polygamy among the Mormons.

As unbiased students and historians of all beliefs have ferreted out the facts, this real and historic undertaking is becoming understood in its proper light and perspective.

Mormonism in a large part is a "restored" religion of the past, a way of living for the present and a plan for the future. All Christians and many non-Christians who believe in ancient Biblical history as it is recorded in the first five books of Moses (or the Pentateuch) in the Old Testament, acknowledge that the patriarchs of those times had more than one wife, or lived in polygamy with divine sanction.

In the early development of the Mormon Church it was divinely revealed to Joseph Smith that this old practice of marriage which was sanctioned in ancient times should be re-established.

At the time polygamy was introduced by Joseph Smith, most of the converts to Mormonism were strict monogamist New England Puritans, and to them it was shocking, and against their customs and training. However, they did accept it as a commandment of God. The practice was restricted to those who had proved themselves capable of maintaining more than one family.

The publicity given to Mormon polygamy, however, has been far out of proportion to all other events that have taken place in the Church's fascinating but relatively short history.

There were never at any time more than three percent of the families of the Church who practiced polygamy.

George Bernard Shaw, famous English writer and a non-Mormon, gave an interesting explanation of the Mormon practice of polygamy in a speech he made in New York City to the Academy of Political Science, at a special meeting in the Metropolitan Opera House, April 11, 1933. He said in part:

"You know, if you study American history — not the old history books; for almost all American histories, until very lately, were mere dustbins of the most mendacious vulgar journalism — but the real history of America, you will be ashamed of it, because the real history of all mankind is shameful. But there is hope in bits of it. I wonder how many of you have ever studied the history of the Latter-day Saints: one of the most extraordinary episodes in the white settlement of the world. You should do so; for it shews Americans doing something for reasons which would astonish me very much if I saw the same thing being done for the same reasons in England.

"There was a time when the Mormons were so few in number that they were in very great danger of being killed by their pious neighbors because their views were unpopular. But they were themselves a very pious people. They were brought up with the strictest old-fashioned ideas with regard to the relations of the sexes and the sanctity of marriage; marriage, of course, being the established monogamous marriage of the Christian west.

"Well, their leader went to these pious men and women and said to them, 'I want you to take to polygamy. I want all you men to have as many wives as you can possibly afford instead of one wife.'

"Think what a terrific thing that was to say to such people! I do not know any more moving passage in literature than that in which Brigham Young describes how, after receiving this appalling order, he met a funeral on his way home and found himself committing the mortal sin of envying the dead. And yet Brigham Young lived to have a very large number of wives according to our ideas, and was to become immortal in history as an American Moses by leading his people through the wilderness into an unpromised land where they founded a great city.

"Now nothing can be more idle, nothing more frivolous, than to imagine that this polygamy had anything to do with personal licentiousness. If Joseph Smith had proposed to the Latter-day Saints that they should live licentious lives, they would have rushed on him and probably anticipated the pious neighbors who presently shot him. The significant point in the case was that the reason he gave them was a purely political reason. He said, "Unless we multiply our numbers, we are lost; and we can multiply our numbers rapidly only by polygamy. And, therefore, whatever our prejudices, whatever our feelings may be, if we are to save the Church of the Latter-day Saints from annihilation by the superior numbers of its enemies in this State, we must take to polygamy.' "

"And they did it. That was the wonderful American thing. A body of Americans were capable of changing their lives and discarding their most deeply rooted ideas for a purely political reason! That makes some of you laugh. I am very glad. Whenever in the search for truth I hit the nail exactly on the head, there is always a laugh at first; but nothing that I shall say tonight is more significant than that illustration of American capacity for political action. . . ."

In their practice of polygamy, the Mormons, at the time, were living according to the religious liberties granted to all Americans by the Constitution of the United States. However, when Congress later enacted laws prohibiting polygamy, the Mormons accepted them, and since October 6, 1890, have neither sanctioned nor practiced polygamy.

They had accepted polygamy as a commandment of God. It had served a worthy purpose. The government of the country to which they pledged allegiance and were citizens abolished polygamy. The Mormons, always believing in upholding the law of the country in which they live, complied with the law and again, by divine sanction, ceased its practice and were therefore "released" from their obligation to comply with the commandment to practice polygamy.

**THE PRACTICE OF POLYGAMY WAS ABOLISHED BY THE MORMON CHURCH IN 1890 AND IS GROUNDS FOR EXCOMMUNICATION.**

# A UNIQUE PROGRAM . . . Genealogy

## Searching for and recording family pedigrees

FROM MANY parts of the world, old records or microfilm copies are sent to the Genealogical Library at Salt Lake City, Utah, where interested Mormons search out their ancestors and build "family trees." The information pertaining to their deceased ancestors plays an important part in connection with ordinances performed in Temples of the Latter-day Saints.

**Geneological Building, Salt Lake City, Utah**

Headquarters of the world-wide activities of records of ancestry. It has the largest Microfilm Library of such records in the world.

Young people throughout the Mormon Church are interested in searching for the names and histories of their ancestors.

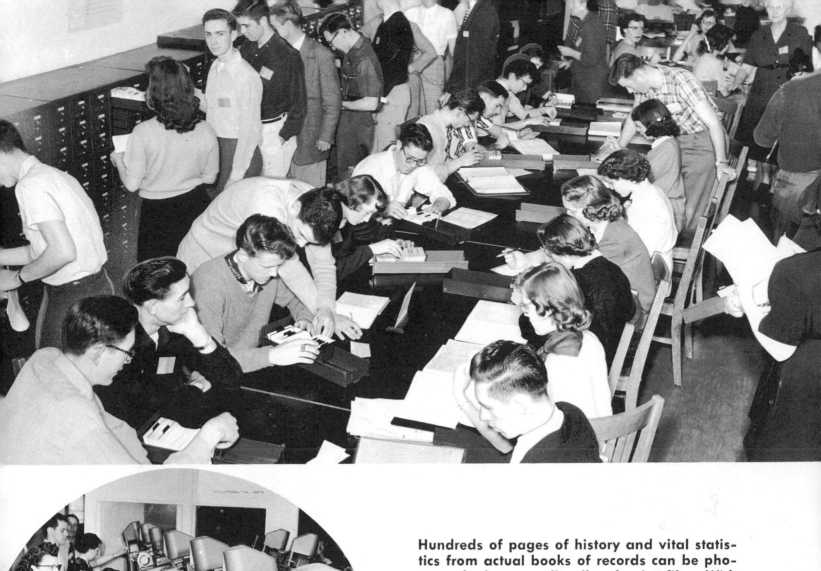

Hundreds of pages of history and vital statistics from actual books of records can be photographed on small rolls of microfilm. With these "view" machines each small filmed page is greatly enlarged for easy study, reading and copying of pertinent information.

# ACTIVITY AND RESPONSIBILITY FOR EVERY MEMBER
## REFLECTS IN THE STRENGTH OF THE "MORMON" CHURCH

Beginning with youth and throughout their lives all members of the Church are taught to know their religion and to assume responsibilities in the Church's tremendous program and activities.

Young people start out with important responsibilities, i.e., class leaders, athletic directors, and officiators in many sacred religious ceremonies.

A representative group of Mormon young women students at the Brigham Young University, Provo, Utah.

A representative group of young men. Hundreds of thousands of similar young men like these throughout the Church have been ordained to, and hold, the Holy Priesthood, or authority to act in God's name to perform many religious ordinances.

At the Brigham Young University Mormons from nearly every state in the United States and many foreign countries attend this Church school, which has an enrollment on the college level of nearly 15,000 students.

## MORMONS ARE MISSIONARY-MINDED

MORMONS (Latter-day Saints) are people from all walks of life, and they take their religion seriously. They try to practice its principles in their daily lives.

One of their endeavors individually and collectively has been and is to share the "Restored" Gospel of Jesus Christ with all people.

Nearly every Mormon has the uniqueness of being a missionary in the sense of always being ready and anxious to explain his religion to all non-Mormons.

A Mormon believes it to be his or her responsibility to spread the new concept of life as it has been revealed from Heaven to Joseph Smith and his successors.

This new concept of life, they believe, will, if followed, bring peace, satisfaction and happiness to mankind.

Mormonism has what it believes to be the answers to man's origin, man's purpose here on earth and man's destiny in a continued existence as an individual identity after this life.

It is a philosophy that gives the Mormon a purposeful life. Birth into this life is a glorious opportunity. Death loses its horror, and the family unit is eternal.

\* \* \* \* \*

## MORMONS ARE GOOD CITIZENS

THEY BELIEVE that the Constitution of the United States is an inspired document.

From the very beginning of the organization of the Mormon Church, women have voted on Church matters.

In the first provisional government set up by the pioneers after their arrival in the Great Salt Lake Valley (State of Deseret 1847-1850) women were also given the franchise to vote on political matters.

Thus the Mormons as a group were among the very first in America to grant women the franchise to vote in both religious and political affairs.

Several Mormons from western states are in both houses of Congress of the United States. Mormons are also to be found in many other high government positions.

Mormons are politically tolerant of those of other faiths. Many of the governors of Utah have been non-Mormons.

# WELCOME

The Mormons, now firmly established in the Rocky Mountains and the West, welcome all to come and see some of the "fruits" of their labors. Under their persistent and intelligent efforts, and in co-operation with other friendly people, they have made the desert truly "blossom as the rose."

The uniqueness of this Land of Color with its fascinating historical background, brings people from all over the world. Many are converts to the Church, many are tourists, and many are just business people passing through, but all are able to see that here is a place and a people that are different. They find proportionately more people living higher ideals — more people translating their religion into daily activities — more people wanting to share their philosophy of life — more people showing a deep-seated purpose of their existence and more people who have found satisfaction and happiness.

## "THIS IS THE PLACE" MONUMENT

(at the mouth of Emigration Canyon, Salt Lake City, Utah)

A fitting memorial to commemorate the historic event which took place approximately at this site on July 24, 1847, when Brigham Young, upon looking over the desolate but peaceful valley of the Great Salt Lake, uttered these words, "THIS IS THE PLACE."

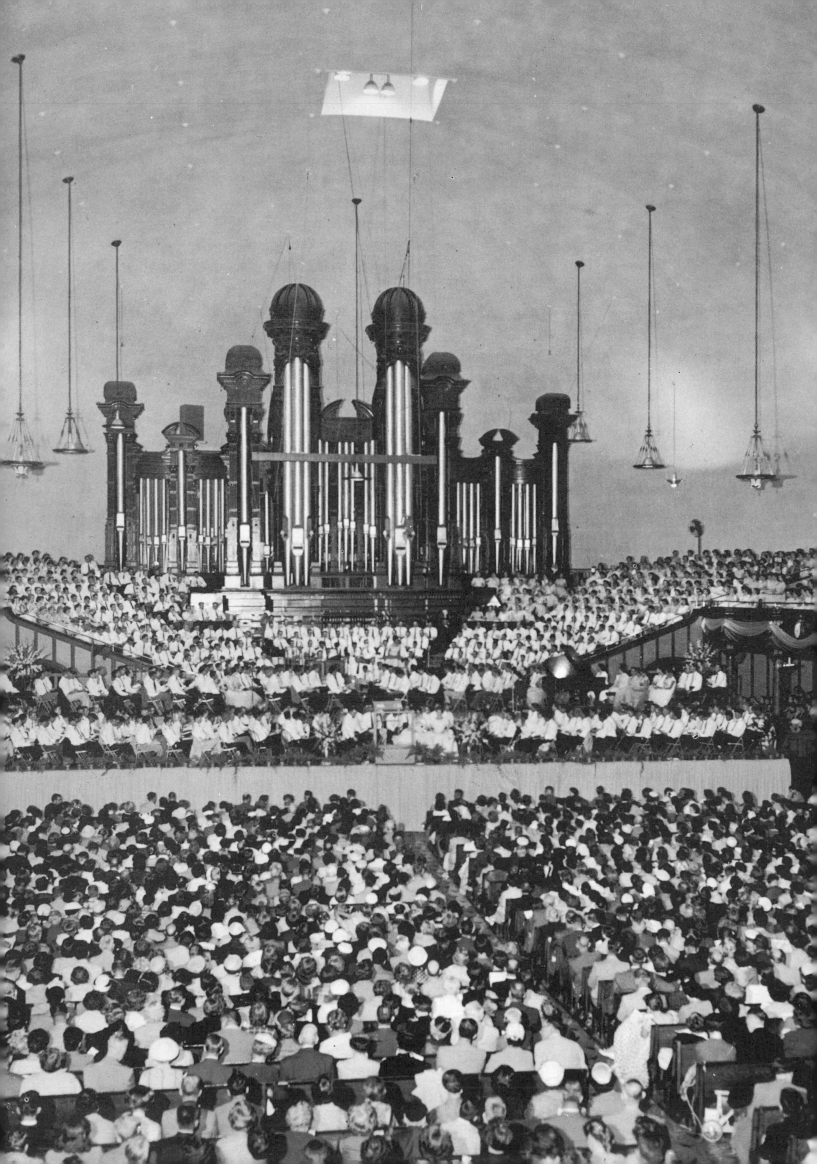

Music is very important to the Mormons. Their hymns are an inspiration, and the development of all musical talent is strongly encouraged. Shown here is a group of young singers and a youth orchestra performing in the famous Tabernacle in Salt Lake City, Utah.

## TEMPLE SQUARE . . . . . In the heart of Salt Lake City

Great numbers of tourists come here each year to hear the "Mormon Story." All take back to their homes a better understanding of the Mormon viewpoint. Many accept it and affiliate themselves with the Church.

Utah has the distinction of having America's first department store, the Zion's Co-operative Mercantile Institution (Z.C.M.I.). This institution was founded in 1868 at Salt Lake City, Utah. This represents the early industry and far-sightedness of Brigham Young and the Mormon Pioneers.

Z.C.M.I.'s modern parking terrace.

**THE HOTEL UTAH** — One of the West's most attractive hotels. It was built by the Mormon Church.

**THE MUNICIPAL BUILDING IN OGDEN . . . Utah's second largest city.**

The 24th of July is a big and important anniversary. Utahns celebrate it in commemoration of the first Pioneers entering the valley, July 24, 1847. This is Main Street on the 24th of July in Salt Lake City, Utah.

**BRIGHTON, SKIING AREA IN THE WASATCH MOUNTAINS**
A Skier's Paradise, near Salt Lake City. There are also many others in Utah.

Building their youth mentally and physically is one of the major programs of the Mormons. Here the Young Men's and Young Women's Mutual Improvement Associations stage a huge dance and musical festival at the University of Utah Stadium in Salt Lake City, Utah.

The Utah State Capitol Building and the Mormon Salt Lake Temple illuminated at night above and daytime view of the State Capitol below. Each symbolizes the great faith of the Pioneers in government and religion.

Salt Lake City, built at first in a place no one else wanted, is now one of America's cleanest and most beautiful cities. Here is seen part of the business section of the city. It is surrounded by an especially attractive residential area with the stately Wasatch Mountains in the background.

The Mormon Tabernacle stands as a monument to the Pioneer spirit of music and worship — built in a wilderness to bring the Mormons together in song and worship. In this building is the famous organ, originally built in 1867, which is world renowned for its tonal qualities.

**Protestant, Catholic and Jewish churches are well represented in Utah, having beautiful chapels, cathedrals, and many buildings for educational and religious services.**

**FIRST METHODIST CHURCH**
Salt Lake City, Utah

**CHRISTIAN SCIENCE CHURCH**
Salt Lake City, Utah

**FIRST PRESBYTERIAN CHURCH**
Salt Lake City, Utah

**ROMAN CATHOLIC CATHEDRAL**
Salt Lake City, Utah

**ZION EVANGELICAL LUTHERAN CHURCH**
Salt Lake City, Utah

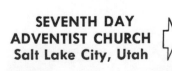

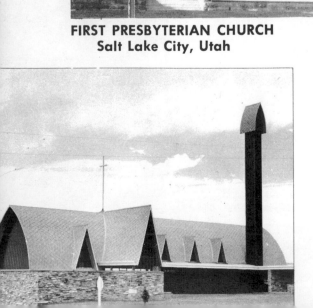

**SEVENTH DAY ADVENTIST CHURCH**
Salt Lake City, Utah

**MASONIC TEMPLE**
Salt Lake City, Utah

**FIRST BAPTIST CHURCH**
Salt Lake City, Utah

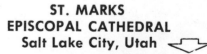

**GREEK ORTHODOX CHURCH**
**HOLY TRINITY**
Salt Lake City, Utah

**JEWISH SYNAGOGUE**
**CONGREGATION MONTEFIORE**
Salt Lake City, Utah

**UNITARIAN CHURCH**
Salt Lake City, Utah

**ST. MARKS**
**EPISCOPAL CATHEDRAL**
Salt Lake City, Utah

**FIRST**
**CONGREGATIONAL CHURCH**
Salt Lake City, Utah

Idaho Falls Temple

Swiss Temple

# AMERICA'S GREAT SALTY INLAND SEA . . .

### . . . near Salt Lake City, Utah

The only body of water in the Americas where you can float like a cork without any effort . . .
The water is 27% salt.

Utah has tremendous deposits of coal and iron ore; the result is a great industry of steel. Shown here is an airview of Geneva Steel Plant near Utah Lake.

# THE BONNEVILLE SALT FLATS

The world's fastest automobile racecourse is located 95 miles west of Salt Lake City, Utah. The Salt Flats area is about 1,000 square miles and forms part of the Great Salt Lake Desert.

# AMERICA'S LARGEST GAME BIRD REFUGE
## ...Northern Utah

## AMERICA'S UNIQUE "COLD WATER" GEYSER

Man started it when drilling for oil; nature has kept it going. It erupts to a height of 200 feet and spouts regularly every hour and ten minutes. It is located near Green River, Utah.

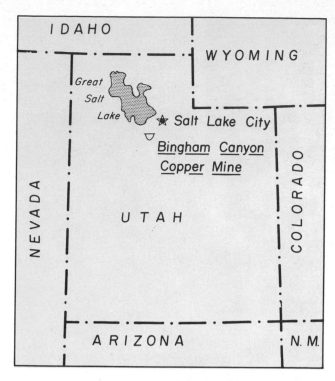

⇩ ## THE WORLD'S LARGEST COPPER MINE
### Bingham, Utah

The Colorado River flows more than two hundred miles through Utah. It has cut deep, and a river expedition down through its steep canyon walls is a thriller.

# DINOSAUR NATIONAL MONUMENT

Located in Northeastern Utah. America's most important natural display of fossilized prehistoric reptile life.

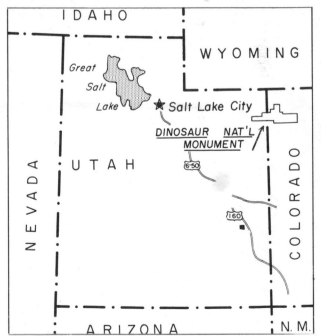

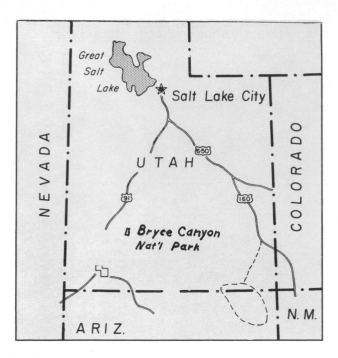

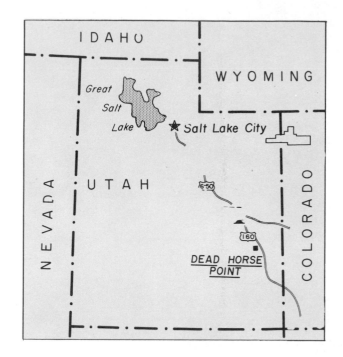

Utah's undeveloped natural scenic resources are tremendous. Here shown is a view of the Colorado River from Dead Horse Point, Utah.

## BRYCE CANYON NATIONAL PARK

With fourteen enormous amphitheaters, sculptured terraces ad pinnacles. The formations have more colors and hues than a rainbow.

**THE GRAND CANYON OF THE COLORADO**

One of nature's greatest, deepest and most spectacular wonders. Located in Arizona, with its north entrance through Utah.

 **MONUMENT VALLEY**

Southeastern Utah and Northeastern Arizona. Part of the Navajo Indian Reservation. Wierd sandstone formations, caused by erosion and wind.

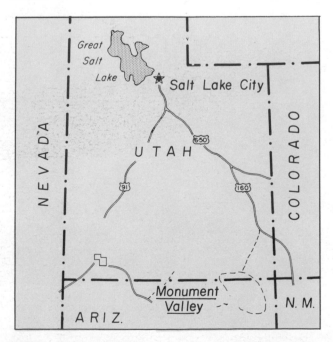

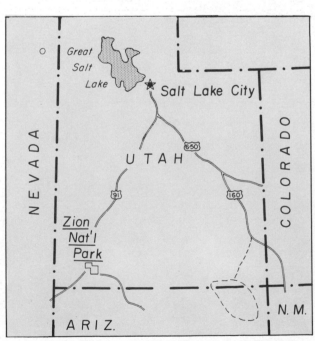

## THE GREAT WHITE THRONE

Zion National Park, Southwest Utah, Mountains of stone in shapes and forms of temples and cathedrals, etc.

## THE WEST RIM TRAIL
### Zion National Park, Southwestern Utah

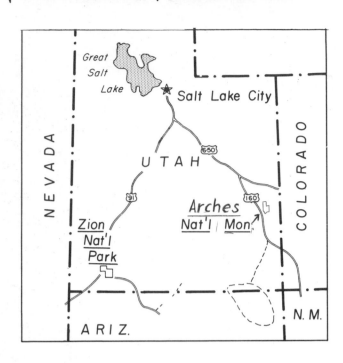

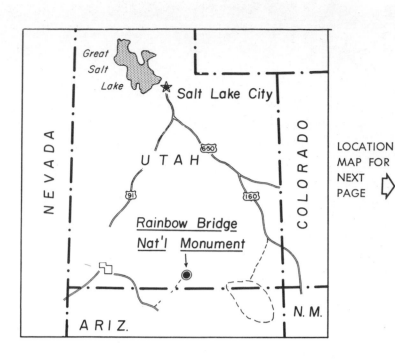

LOCATION MAP FOR NEXT PAGE

## DOUBLE ARCH IN UTAH'S ARCHES NATIONAL MONUMENT

**This area has dozens of huge natural arches, natural bridges and unique erosive formations.**

UTAH'S RAINBOW NATIONAL MONUMENT

Nature's largest, most beautiful and graceful natural bridge,
309 feet high. The National Capitol Building at Washington,
D. C. could stand under its span with 22 feet to spare.